Fishers of Men
Discipleship Ministry For Relational Evangelism

http://fishersofmen.org/

Leadership Training

For the *Fishers of Men* Series

"Come, follow me," Jesus said,
"and I will make you fishers of men."

At once they left their nets and followed him.

Matthew 4:19-20

Scott J. Visser

We value your input.

Please send your comments about this book and series to info@fishersofmeninc.org

Thank you!

Fishers of Men Leadership Training

Copyright © 2010 by Scott J. Visser

Request for information should be addressed to:

Scott Visser
7755 N Carefree Drive, Whitehall, MI 49461

Books may be ordered at http://fishersofmeninc.org/

ISBN – 978-0-9826219-4-3

Scripture taken from the Holy Bible, New International Version ®, NIV ®
Copyright © 1973, 1978, 1984 by Biblica Inc.™
Used by permission of Zondervan. All rights reserved worldwide. WWW.ZONDERVAN.COM
The "NIV" and "New International Version" are trademarks registered in the United States Patent and Trademark Offices by Biblica Inc.™

All rights reserved. No part of this publication may be reproduced, stored in a retrieval system, or transmitted in any form or by any means – electronic, mechanical, photocopy, or any other method – except for brief quotations for promotional purposes – without the prior permission of the publisher.

Interior design by Scott Visser

Interior layout by Juan Garnica

Book covers by Richard E. Williams

Publisher: Fishers of Men Inc.

Acknowledgments

I am grateful for the many people who helped with this project.

Let's start with my original *Fishers of Men* class in Linton, Indiana.

Do you remember our first talks about relational evangelism? Your courage to be real even when it exposed our fears, faults and insecurities was priceless in the development of this project. Your honesty gave us a starting point from which we could plot our course to where the Lord was leading us. The God who gives grace to the humble gave much grace to us! He used you to help give birth to this discipleship ministry.

Michael Jaffe, Professor of Evangelism and Discipleship at Central Bible College in Springfield, Missouri

Your insights, encouragement and willingness to challenge my thinking raised the standard of this work.

Paul Smith, General Editor of Gospel Publishing House

Your critiques of an early manuscript helped cut clutter and clarify my writing style.

My Board: Ken Gothman and Dawn Garvelink

Thanks for the many hours of support.

Thanks to those who helped prepare this project for print:

Jean Van Houten, copy editor
Juan Garnica, formatting

Richard E. Williams, Possibilities Productions @ possiblemedia.com

The project would still be in my laptop if it were not for you.

My wife, Gin Visser

Your faith, love, patience, perseverance and support was (and is) priceless to me!

The Holy Spirit

Without Your conviction, encouragement and guidance this work would have never been started, let alone completed.

To all who desire to prepare
so that you know enough,
dare enough and care enough
to catch men's hearts for Christ.

Roll up your sleeves.

It is time to get started.

CONTENTS

Chapter 1	The Case for Relational Evangelism	9
Chapter 2	Beginning With the End in Mind	17
Chapter 3	Equipping the Team	22
Chapter 4	A Reality Check	27
Chapter 5	The Preacher, the Teacher, and the Coach	31
Chapter 6	Making a New Factory for the New Product	37
Chapter 7	Discipleship Dynamics	39
Chapter 8	Discipleship Structures	67
Chapter 9	Discipleship Tools	95
Chapter 10	Fitting it all together	118
Chapter 11	Leadership Skills	123
Chapter 12	Overcoming Discipleship Hang-ups	137
Chapter 13	Starting a Fishers of Men Group	143

Is *Fishers of Men* For You?

Answer the Following Questions

"0" means you strongly disagree. "5" indicates that you strongly agree.

1. I desire to obey Christ and make disciples. _____

2. Relational evangelism sounds better to me than "stranger evangelism." _____

3. I would like interactive experiential discipleship rather than passive listening. _____

4. I would like to learn about discipleship dynamics, structures and tools. _____

5. I would like to be part of a group that focuses on outreach. _____

6. I would like coaching rather than just talking and listening. _____

7. I would like to equip myself and others so that we become people who know enough, dare enough and care enough to lead others to faith in Christ and help them grow in Christ. _____

8. I want to follow Christ and truly become a fisher of men for Him. _____

9. I would like to try a fresh, new, biblical approach to discipleship. _____

10. I would like to stretch out of my comfort zones and take on a discipleship challenge with others. _____

Total _____

Score	Comments
0-9	You do not want to read this book.
10-19	Perhaps this book will change your mind.
20-29	This book will light new fires for evangelism.
30-39	You are going to like this book.
40-50	You are going to love this book.

Chapter 1

The Case for Relational Evangelism

Relationship is one of the strongest influences in the world. People will sooner follow a friend than they will follow the preacher. In fact, the pull of relationship is so strong that many will turn from what is right and follow what is wrong in order to keep a relationship.

We are called to turn people to God. It is a daunting task and we seek the best methods to bring the most success. Evangelists work with teams to reach the masses. Churches present powerful evangelistic dramas and draw in hundreds. Groups engage in servant evangelism to win good will and give their church a good name. Others take the confrontational approach, addressing strangers in public places, confronting their sin and urging them to faith in Christ.

> **Relationship is one of the strongest influences in the world.**

Many like myself have engaged in all these efforts. And the truth is, whatever the method, new converts still need relationships. Otherwise, when the dust settles after all the work, few remain connected. They need people who know enough and care enough to help them continue to grow and walk with Christ.

This book will help you prepare yourself and others to become those kind of people. Other styles of evangelism certainly have their place. However, this ministry prepares people for relational evangelism. Here are several reasons why:

1. **Jesus believes in relational evangelism.**

> ... they will never follow a stranger; in fact, they will run away from him because they do not recognize a stranger's voice. *John 10:5*

Jesus taught about the importance of relationship in the parable of the Good Shepherd in John 10. A good shepherd gets to know the sheep and calls them by name. He is there for them. He looks out for their best interest. He leads them to green pastures and quiet waters. When a wolf attempts to prey on them, it must first get through him. Sheep will follow a man like that.

Jesus also taught what kind of person sheep will not follow. He said:

> "They will never follow a stranger; in fact, they will run away from him because they do not recognize a stranger's voice." *John 10:5*

His point was obvious: Sheep are not influenced by strangers. Sheep do not trust strangers. In fact, instead of running *to* them, they run *from* them. It is the same way with people. "Stranger evangelism" is not received well because people do not trust strangers enough to follow them. They may respond to an altar call. However, most do not respond well to the follow-up later. Why? There is no relationship.

> **Sheep run from strangers.**
> **So do people.**

Here's the question:

> Why do we continually attempt to make quick converts of strangers when Jesus said this method does not work?

Jesus taught relational evangelism. He also put it into practice. He not only died for sinners: He lived for them. He wept in prayer for them. He healed them. He taught them. At times He fed them. He gave of His time, His heart and power and never charged a dime. He ate dinner with tax collectors, forgave and delivered an adulteress, and talked with the likes of Samaritan women. In fact, Jesus was so relational that He was accused in contemptible terms by the religious leaders as being "a friend of tax collectors and 'sinners.'" (Matthew 11:19)

Whatever He did – it sure worked! The way He loved people and told them the truth radically changed their hearts and lives. The Samaritan woman became the first woman evangelist. She went back to her town telling everyone, "Come, see a man who told me everything I ever did. Could this be the Christ?" (John 4:29) The adulteress lived to tell about His mercy that said, "Go now and leave your life of sin." (John 8:11) The tax collector, Zacchaeus, while hosting Jesus in his home, stood up and declared to the Lord and his many guests, "Look, Lord! Here and now I give half of my possessions to the poor, and if I have cheated anybody out of anything, I will pay back four times the amount." (Luke 19:8)

Christ's holy love changed people's hearts. It was not just His power. It was not just His truth. It was His love. It was His willingness and even desire for relationship that turned people to Him. Jesus changed lives through relational evangelism.

2. The Apostle Paul believed in relational evangelism.

> We loved you so much that we were delighted to share with you not only the gospel of God but our lives as well, because you had become so dear to us. *1 Thessalonians 2:8*

Paul's message to the Thessalonians was not just that *God* loved them. Paul and his team loved them too! They gave their lives as well as the Gospel. Their words and their deeds proved that these people had become dear to them.

In relational evangelism, new people become dear to us. They may not be dear at first, but as we pray for them, care for them and share with them our hearts become attached to theirs. People like being dear to people, and – it just makes sense – they will comprehend that they are dear to God when they realize that they are dear to His children. If they feel our love, they will more quickly believe in His. Maybe the term, "God loves you" will not seem so trite to people when it is accompanied by our love. Maybe they will recognize His love in us if we show His love in relationship.

Relational evangelism was quite a change of heart for this former Pharisee named Paul. Pharisees loved their religion. They loved their holy temple. They loved their beautiful robes and the admiration they received from people. They loved their appearance of righteousness. They just didn't love people – especially sinners. They were quick to criticize and condemn. They knew very little about showing mercy and offering help. Christ's love changed all that in Paul's heart. Now people were dear to him. Now he loved them enough to share his life as well as the gospel.

> **In relational evangelism, new people become dear to us.**

3. God believes in relational evangelism.

> For God so loved the world that he gave his one and only Son, that whoever believes in him shall not perish but have eternal life.
> *John 3:16*

God, the Maker of heaven and earth and the Judge of all creation loved us so much that He gave His own Son to pay our penalty so that we could have restored relationship with Him and enjoy fellowship with Him forever in heaven. Can you imagine loving someone so much that you would give your son to die for them? There is no greater love.

People are badly mistaken when they see God as someone who is distant and far away. They don't understand that "God is spirit, and his worshipers must worship in spirit and in truth." (John 4:24) Spirit is invisible. God visits their conscience on a regular basis and bids them to repent – to turn from sin and to turn to Him and be saved. Some will and some won't but the point is this: Even though people cannot *see* God, they also cannot *escape* God. He haunts men's hearts. Though His presence may incite fear and agitation to the wicked because He is displeased with them, if they repent, He will forgive them, clean them up and reinstate them into His good graces. He continually draws the hearts of His children closer to him. It is not God's fault that people would rather do other things than fellowship with God through His Word and His Spirit. His Spirit is available to us every day. My friend, you cannot get any more relational than that!

4. Relational evangelism combines truth and love

>Instead, speaking the truth in love, we will in all things grow up into him who is the Head, that is, Christ. *Ephesians 4:15*

Consider these dynamics between love and truth. People need truth, but many people are not influenced by truth without love. People need love, but love without truth does not lead people out of spiritual darkness. They need truth. They need direction. They need leadership in their lives. So which is more important – truth or love? They are inseparable. Real love tells the truth. Real truth reveals God's love. Love and truth is a powerful divine combination of influences that changes people's lives. Relationship communicates love. Evangelism shares the truth of Christ. Relational evangelism offers love and truth together.

5.   Relational evangelism requires risk but bears better results.

The truth is, most of us would rather reach out to strangers than friends with the message of Christ. It's less risky. Who wants to tell a friend that he is a sinner in need of a Savior? We might offend him. Worse yet, we might lose our friend. There is less to lose by talking to strangers. If we offend them, we have not lost anything.

Relational evangelism requires much more work, care, and commitment than those encounters where we ride into people's lives, offer momentary friendship, share the Good News, lead them in a prayer, then mount our white horse and ride off into the sunset. What is that? I'm sorry. This will not sound polite but it is a "one night stand." It's a short-term love relationship. It is like making a baby and then not bothering to take care of it. It's wrong. People need the Gospel: They also need relationship. They need relationship with God. They also need relationship with His kids. New Christians need more than a pamphlet and talk about going to church. They need to be invited over for dinner. They need friends who will walk with them.

Though relational evangelism requires more, it also gives more. It offers new loving and *eternal* relationships. It brings rich fulfillment, love and joy from the extreme privilege of being a part of God's plan to bring lost people back into His family. As our heart becomes like God's heart, we also will love them deeply and experience the pure joy of sinless fellowship with them in heaven. There is no reward better than that!

**People need the Gospel.
They also need relationship.**

---

6. Relationship is one of the strongest influences in the world.

> And now these three remain: faith, hope and love. But the greatest of these is love. *1 Corinthians 13:12-13*

As I stated before, people will sooner follow a friend than they will the preacher. In fact, the pull of relationship is so strong that many will turn from what is right and follow what is wrong in order to keep a relationship. A man may have right doctrine and may know the right way to live but if he has no relationship with those he hopes to lead, he will be very frustrated. Why? He has no influence. They will not follow him.

This is why relational evangelism is better than offering tracts to strangers. It is better than a one-time encounter. It is better than handing out free water to a crowd. It is better than a program. These outreach approaches are not bad things. In fact, they are good tools when used correctly as part of the process of reaching people. However, they are not substitutes for real love shown in real relationship that continually reaches and nurtures others in Christ.

7. Relational Evangelism obeys one of God's greatest commands.

> Love your neighbor as yourself. *Mark 12:31*

Relational evangelism is evangelism with personal love. Love works to win hearts rather than just arguments. Love seeks to engraft new relationships into our life rather than just put more people in the pew. It's personal. It cares. It moves us to care for our neighbor next door and the one who has been ripped-off, bruised, beat up and left for dead by the devil. Love is compassionate. It is like the Good Samaritan. It does not allow us to walk by but rather to take action even at the cost of our convenience, our time and our money. God so loved that He gave. We should also. If His Spirit is truly in us, we will.

Relational evangelism does not look for the preacher or some program in organized religion to care. Relational evangelism moves *us* to care. As we learn to truly care, we will go out of our way to help people learn how to be reconciled with God and experience a love relationship with Him.

May God make us more like Paul, more like Christ, and more like Himself. May He grant us repentance so that we love our things less and love lost people more. May they become dear to us and that dearness move us to lay our lives down for them and reach out to them in relational evangelism. I pray you sense this conviction in your heart. If you do, read on! We are only getting started!

> **Relational evangelism is evangelism with personal love.**

Chapter 2

Beginning

With the End in Mind

"Come, follow me," Jesus said, "and I will make you fishers of men."
Matthew 4:19

Now that we understand the case for relational evangelism, let's consider how to begin. How do we prepare for this kind of outreach?

The first step is to begin with the end in mind. When people see a clear picture of the desired goal, they can pursue it with clarity and confidence. When people know what they are aiming for, they can know whether they hit or missed the target.

Jesus prepared His first disciples by creating a clear picture of what men would become if they followed Him. Men who once caught fish would now catch the hearts of men for the Kingdom of God. Furthermore, rather than eating the catch, this new kind of fishing would be a rescue mission. The team would lead others out of the polluted waters of this world and deliver them into the fresh, life-giving waters of the Kingdom of God.

While we are developing the picture, let's make sure we are clear on one very important point: The term "men" refers to "mankind." It includes women. It includes boys. It includes girls. It includes every age from the youngest to the oldest. Jesus did not reach out to only men. He reached out to everyone.

My wife and sisters thought I should call the ministry, "Shoppers for Women!" I laughed and told them to write their own book! I used Jesus' phrase instead of theirs. However, be assured that when Christ raised up His first disciples, His intention was to save and include all in His kingdom. He desired all to be the light of the world, the salt of the earth and fishers of men for Him.

He has the same picture in mind for us today – and nothing less. Becoming a faithful church-goer is fine but it is not His end product. Seeing the Lord help us with our problems is a wonderful benefit of being in God's family, but there is more to following Christ than that. Becoming mature and holy is part of God's plan but it does not stop there. Experiencing God's presence in worship and prayer is an absolute thrill for those who discover this treasure but there is more that God has in mind for us. Being busy in the work of God's church is far better than being busy with the less important things of this world. However, sometimes even that can be a substitute for the real thing God desires. All these things are good and even godly. Christ still has the same end in mind for us that He had for His original disciples. Jesus intends for us to become fishers of men in our generation.

> **Jesus intends for us to become fishers of men in our generation.**

While we are getting the picture, let's make sure we properly understand Christ's heart. He is still very concerned for the lost. I dare say He weeps for them. Have you pictured that in your mind? Reaching people's hearts for Christ is not merely an aspiration to a godly ideal. It certainly is not as casual as going out and fishing for fish. How would we feel if our child was lost? That is how the Lord feels.

If we don't get this picture and do not comprehend our Lord's heart, we become part of a horrible scene – the lost continue to perish while Christ's followers focus on lesser things.

The *Fishers of Men* series helps people get the right picture. It prepares people so that they know enough, dare enough, and care enough to share enough to catch men's hearts for Christ. These people become a team - an evangelist cell group whose goal is, "Each one to reach one and help them grow in their faith."

Once trained, they focus on actual outreach rather than more learning. They pray, strategize, and mobilize to reach the lost for Christ. They give account for their progress and help each other stay focused. They make it their obedient goal to "catch fish." They dare to look at the stringer. They change tactics if present efforts are not working. They measure, recognize and celebrate progress together.

Once people are reached for Christ, one or more team members connect relationally with them. They also help them get to know Jesus better by reading about Him together in one of the gospels. The goal is help them find out who Christ is, what He did and what He said. As they get to know Jesus better, they respect Him more, love Him more and trust Him more. These dynamics influence people to follow Him. It works from the inside-out rather than the outside-in. Religious rules cannot do that. Expectations from others, or even one's self, cannot do that. Only a relationship with Jesus that is infused with respect, love and trust can bring people into a reconciled relationship with God and a transformed life.

As you can imagine, team members may be at different stages with people in the outreach process. In fishing terms, some may be getting out in the boat and onto the water for the very first time. They are getting out of their usual routine and connecting with others who do not know the Lord. They are "getting their feet wet" so to speak. They're making new friends, building the relationship and establishing trust. Others are actively casting and finding which lure and presentation creates the bite. They are telling others why they are "hooked on Jesus" and persuading them to do the same. Others are setting the hook and making their point regarding who Jesus is and what He said. Some will be in the angling process. They have hooked someone's attention and are in the process of pulling their heart nearer to God. Others have pulled their new friend completely on board and are now orienting them to the fresh water of God's Kingdom of righteousness, peace and joy in the Holy Spirit. They are helping them learn the basic lifestyle truths about repentance, faith, and water baptism. Of course, some converts will already be enthusiastic about helping others come to Christ. Once the new Christians are firmly connected relationally to the Lord and to other Christians, team members help others. No matter what stage a team member is at, they have the group to pray with them, offer suggestions and encouragement, and to help them stay focused on fishing for men.

That is the end in mind. That is the kind of team this discipleship ministry develops. In manufacturing terms, this is the new product that will come off the end of the assembly line.

Now that we understand the desired end product, let's consider how to properly equip ourselves to achieve it.

Here is the end in mind: people who know enough, dare enough, and care enough to share enough to catch men's hearts for Christ.

Chapter 3

Equipping the Team

All Scripture is God-breathed and is useful for teaching, rebuking, correcting and training in righteousness, [17]so that the man of God may be thoroughly equipped for every good work. *2 Timothy 3:16*

The *Fishers of Men* series provides step-by-step training in eight key areas to equip God's people for the good work of relational evangelism. Here they are:

1. The first step helps people to commit to follow Christ and become fishers of men for Him. It prepares them to make a serious commitment to training for outreach. Rather than the typical teaching format, students engage in a variety of small group discussions, study and prayer. Through these the group gains a real sense of taking this journey together rather than trying to do it alone.

2. The second step helps Christians help others know who Jesus is. When people don't understand who Christ is, they don't put much stock in what He said. After all, to them, Jesus is just one of many opinions. This study prepares Christians to show Jesus as God's Messiah promised beforehand by His prophets. When people realize who He is, they will listen to what He said.

3. The third step prepares people to tell God's Good News in clear, non-religious terms. It goes beyond leading someone in a sinner's prayer. It is more than offering a "get out of hell free" card or an eternal life fire

4. insurance program. The goal is to lead people into a reconciled relationship to God through repentance from sin and faith in Christ.

5. Step four helps people tell the story of their personal journey with God. As they share how God actively works in their life, others will relate and be encouraged to let God work in their heart also.

6. Step five prepares people to effectively approach God in intercession for the lost. It also equips them to come against the powers of darkness on behalf of the lost. Relationship is not the only factor in reaching the lost. Intercession and spiritual warfare are required.

7. Step six helps people answer the hard questions about God and life. People don't understand why God allows certain things – like suffering, death, and hypocrites. If Christians can help unbelievers turn these stumbling blocks into stepping stones, they will have done them a great service.

8. Step seven shows people how to receive the spiritual power needed in order to be witnesses for Christ. Training alone is only part of the process. Christ's followers were first discipled. However, even with their training, they still had to be empowered by God's promised Holy Spirit. So do we. This step will teach about that power and show people how to receive fresh empowerment from God on a daily basis.

9. Step eight trains people how to make steps of spiritual progress with others. It starts with building trust and relationship. It helps prepare the person and the atmosphere so that people can comfortably get real with God and each other.

Each of these steps are training units. These units are academic. Real learning takes place. They are spiritual. Real convictions and faith are developed. Last but not least, they are highly relational. Real relationships are built right in the classroom setting. How is that so? You will see in the pages ahead.

Each unit requires approximately eight weeks to complete and is geared to help people not only hear the information but actually learn it They are placed in a logical order as described above. However, they may also be taught individually or as a stand-alone unit. Their order may be revised. The series preview on the next two pages provides an overview of each.

FISHERS OF MEN
Discipleship Ministry For Relational Evangelism

SERIES PREVIEW

Unit Two

Proclaiming The Promised Messiah

Unit Goal

To prepare to proclaim Christ as God's Messiah promised by His prophets - because people need to realize who Jesus is before they will listen to what He said.

Unit Four

Telling My Story

Unit Goal

To learn how to confidently and competently present the Good News of Christ by sharing my testimony with others.

Unit Three

Telling God's Good News

Unit Goal

To become a faithful messenger of God's Good News and to help people be reconciled to God by putting their faith in Jesus, His Son.

Unit One

Committing to His Call

Unit Goal

To join together and prepare our hearts to hear and follow Christ's call to be fishers of men.

> "Come, follow me," Jesus said, "and I will make you fishers of men." At once they left their nets and followed him.
> - Matthew 4:19-20

Chapter 3   Equipping the Team

Unit Eight

Unit Six

Relational Evangelism

**Answering
The Hard Questions**

Unit Goal

Unit Goal

To learn how to build bridges of relationship, trust and influence so that people become more likely to receive God's Good News.

To learn how to help people turn life's stumbling blocks into God's stepping stones so they draw near to Him.

Graduation and Outreach

Unit Seven

**Empowered
by the Spirit**

Unit Five

Unit Goal

**Intercession and
Spiritual Warfare**

To gain understanding of God's promised power and to receive a fresh endowment of His power for the purpose of being Christ's witnesses.

Unit Goal

To learn how to approach God in intercession and know how to oppose spiritual powers of darkness on behalf of others.

OUR MISSION
We are getting prepared to follow Jesus and to catch men's hearts for Christ – one step at a time.

Therefore, since we are surrounded by such a great cloud of witnesses, let us throw off everything that hinders and the sin that so easily entangles. And let us run with perseverance the race marked out for us. *Hebrews 12:1*

Chapter 4

A Reality Check

Anyone in the teaching or preaching ministry for any length of time knows that teaching alone does not necessarily produce results. Many people have already heard lessons on these things and still have never led one person to Christ. Many Christians have gone to church their whole life and still have not become successful fishers of men. If the church were a factory, sooner or later we might dare come to the conclusion that our process is not creating the end product Christ described. We are producing defective parts! Worse yet, no one is taking notice. If someone does take notice, they might be criticized for being negative. Who's going to blame the teachers? They are doing their best. Who's going to complain to the people. It would not likely be well-received. However, the truth is, if most Christian education institutions were car manufacturers, we would have been out of business years ago. When cars are defective, someone eventually demands a product recall.

We are not building cars. We are making disciples. What should we do? Should we continue with the same procedures and hope that our end product will improve on its own? That won't work. If we continue teaching as usual, we will get the same product as usual.

> **If we continue teaching as usual, we will get the same product as usual.**

Let's face it. Many sense the problem. They just don't know the solution.

If our end product is not working the way it was intended to work, we should take a look at the present educational factory in the church. Let's do that right now.

Our most popular form of education happens on Sunday mornings. We preach God's Word. Some dynamics of preaching vary from person-to-person. The general dynamics are the same. One man communicates God's Word to the congregation, generally seated in rows to maximize the seating space. All the attention is pointed toward the messenger. The message generally lasts anywhere between twenty minutes to an hour.

The general emphasis of preaching usually falls into the following categories:

- It builds up the believer in the knowledge of Christ and God's Word.
- It encourages the downcast. It brings correction of sin.
- It presents the Good News and bids people to turn to Christ.
- It promotes vision for the days ahead.

All are scriptural purposes. Furthermore, preaching allows one man to communicate a large amount of information in a relatively brief time to a large group of people. He prays and prepares during the week and then feeds back to the congregation what he has spiritually digested. His goal is to make his words easy for others to comprehend and assimilate – like a mother providing milk for her young. It is a scriptural practice.

The problem is, preaching alone is not effective. While it may inspire and feed the sheep, it lacks in other areas. One of the greatest weaknesses of this ministry style is how little people remember. What did your preacher preach three weeks ago? There. I made my point.

> **The problem is, preaching alone is not effective.**

Chapter 4   A Reality Check

Still, it is a valid form of ministry in the church. I don't remember what I ate three weeks ago either but if I decided to consider eating to be in vain, I wouldn't live long enough to forget about it!

Let's look at our second most popular form of education – teaching. Teaching is usually done in smaller groups and may cater to the group's age, interests and needs. Teaching usually instructs people how to deal with various aspects of life and serving God. Teachers often include the class members in conversation during the lesson. The seating is arranged in rows for larger groups or in circles or at tables for smaller groups.

The commitment level of the teacher and the students is usually higher than the average commitment level of the Sunday morning congregation. The less-committed do not attend classes or small groups. Therefore, teachers sometimes provide more learning tools than the preacher. People may use a study book or take notes. The pace is usually a little slower and there is potential for more interaction. These dynamics help people internalize God's Word more deeply and remember it longer.

Teaching dynamics outside the church are far stronger than those inside the church. In schools, teachers are expected to teach specific information depending on the class and the age group. Students are also expected to learn. Their attendance and progress is not voluntary. Elements of review, homework, quizzes, tests, scores, and grades for graduation are employed to promote and measure progress. This creates accountability and the potential for success and joy or failure and disappointment. Most churches do not engage in these dynamics for fear that people would not attend their classes.

That is what the average church has in its educational factory. It is certainly better than nothing. It may produce good people. It feeds people. It often produces consistent churchgoers. Some may even desire to share their faith. However, it falls short of producing people who know enough, dare enough, and care enough to share enough to men's hearts for Christ. The sad result is our churches do not grow. The much sadder result is people are perishing!

That is our reality check. We need something more.

> **Teaching dynamics outside the church
> are far stronger than those inside the church.**

Chapter 5

The Preacher, the Teacher, and the Coach

So far, we have used the imagery of fishing and factories. Imagine now if the goal were to create a winning church football team using only our present models of preparation. The preacher would passionately prepare several sermons. His first talk would tout the benefits football brings to the community. His second message might highlight the need for unity and teamwork. And finally, his third talk celebrates the glories and the thrill of success.

Then he sends the congregation out to play another team.

Unfortunately, they get creamed. They lose so badly it's an embarrassment. It is so embarrassing, no one even wants to talk about it. Furthermore, no one wants to play again.

In response to the agony, future sermons include other topics like "How to deal with wounds and discouragement." Later on, the preacher preaches about our final victory in Christ. That's all good. People are more than glad to come and hear him preach. But no one wants to get out on the field.

The teacher in the congregation sees the need (at least part of it) and creates a teaching series titled, "How to Play Football." Lesson 1 covers basic objectives and rules of play. Lesson 2 explains key positions and their basic roles. They learn who blocks, who throws, who catches and so on. Lesson 3 teaches fundamental football skills. It includes topics like: how to hike the ball, block the defense, throw a pass, catch the ball and run with the ball.

Then the teacher sends them out to play.

They still get creamed.

You get the picture. They don't just need information. They need practice. They need conditioning. They need a place where they can do it wrong until they get it right. And, all the while they need someone who is passionate enough about the game and their progress, to encourage, cheer, connect, and possibly even get emotional. It means he cares. They need a coach.

Evangelism is like a football game. The competition is real. Our opposing team is Satan and his squad. We are competing with him for the hearts of men. We are pressing to get their hearts over God's goal line. The devil's team is pushing them towards his. They use influences of deception, fear, lust, pride, greed, anger, bitterness, unbelief and the like. We promote the faith, hope, love, forgiveness, righteousness, peace and joy that come from Christ. Satan's team is well-trained and not nice. The competition is intense. The score lasts for eternity. We better get ready. We need preachers to inspire and encourage. We need teachers to teach. However, we desperately need coaches to coach.

> **We desperately need coaches to coach.**

Over the years, we have used comforting jargon to cover up our lack of training, coaching and practice. We say things like:

- "All we do is plant the seed. It is up to God to save."
- "Just trust in Jesus."
- "The battle is the Lord's – not ours."

It's not that these encouragements are not true. However, if these words inadvertently provide a comfortable substitute for dedication, effort, and practice, we have a real problem. The ugly truth is, most people are not good at sharing their faith because they have not invested the time and effort required to become good. Most leaders don't dare to point out the problem for fear of appearing mean. So instead, we comfort them. However, we never fix the problem because we don't dare identify the problem. That dynamic would never be allowed in professional sports. If God's people were even half as dedicated to becoming skilled with God's Word as boys and men become skilled in sports, we would be an incredible force to reckon with. Instead, we comfort incompetence rather than correct it. Don't get me wrong. I realize that there are other factors involved other than the believer's personal ability. Some may say that I am too hard on myself or others for thinking this way. I don't think so.

I wish I could infiltrate the devil's team and preach our comfort jargon to them. If I could comfort them in such a way and remove any pressure of rightful responsibility to prepare, fight the good fight, and do their best to be workmen approved, maybe they would become less intense. In fact, I would buy them all comfortable chairs and tell them effort is no longer necessary. Instead of practice, they can sit and listen to me talk. All they need to do is trust their lord for the victory. He will do all the work. I would serve them coffee, donuts, and pink lemonade. I would sing nice songs and promote a casual atmosphere. Who knows? Sooner or later they might get as soft as we are.

Then, at the same time, I would give Christ's team a few revelations no one told them before. I would tell them that Ephesians 6:17 says that God's Word is the sword of the Spirit. It is mighty. I can cut through powers of darkness. However, swords in the sheath do not win battles. Furthermore, swords do not swing themselves. We must swing the sword. I would tell them that if they did more than occasionally watch the preacher swing his sword and learned how to swing it themselves, God would use them to win some victories.

Then we would practice using God's sword. Christians would learn how to parry – to defend their faith with Scripture rather than their own words. They would learn how to grip tightly to God's sword so the devil or others could not easily knock it out with some deceptive argument or philosophy. Let's face it, if God's people don't have a strong personal grip on God's Word, they will not do well against the devil's deception. In the war of words and debates where our

tongues are the sword, many Christians lose every time. In fact, they avoid battles every day for fear of losing them. God's people avoid the battle because they are unskilled and unprepared to personally win the battle. It's time to train God's people to pick up God's sword. When people practice more, they will win more. When more people are skilled with God's Word, more people will be won for Christ.

> **When people practice more, they will win more.**

Here is a concept we must understand. Practice is the bridge that helps people cross the chasm between hearing truth and walking out the truth in their lives. Teachers and preachers only talk. Coaches practice. Coaches mobilize the team to play. Quality coaches raise up capable teams. May God raise up leaders who will coach God's people! May the Lord raise up men to provide coaching manuals instead of just sermon notes and teaching manuals. Each unit of the *Fishers of Men* series is one of those manuals.

Though we use the terms coaching, mentoring and apprenticeship, Jesus called it discipleship. Here is how he described it to His first disciples:

> "All authority in heaven and on earth has been given to me. [19]Therefore go and make disciples of all nations, baptizing them in the name of the Father and of the Son and of the Holy Spirit, [20]and teaching them to obey everything I have commanded you. And surely I am with you always, to the very end of the age."
> *Matthew 28:18*

Luke records the disciples' response to Christ's great commission in the Book of Acts. Once they received the promised power of the Holy Spirit those who were discipled, coached, and trained by Christ carried out His call with skill, spiritual authority, compassion and effectiveness. They knew enough. They cared enough. They dared enough. They spoke up and shared enough so that others found out about Jesus and received Him into their hearts. The first disciples were coached and then they effectively coached others. The results were this: The Kingdom of God made awesome advances against the powers of darkness.

Now, with Christ's help, we are to coach the team. As the first Christians reached their generation, we must reach ours. Just as football players become completely immersed mentally, emotionally, and physically into football, we are to influence, lead, and coach people to be completely immersed (baptized) into the name, the person and the purposes of Jesus our Lord. As football players become so dedicated that they "eat, drink and sleep football," we must instill the same passion for the Kingdom of God. Baptizing people's bodies in water must be accompanied by baptizing their heads and hearts into Jesus and His Spirit. Otherwise they missed the whole point. They just got wet.

That's the thing about coaches. They don't allow the team to miss the point. They put the point into practice together. That is the difference between the preacher, the teacher and the coach.

If this conviction is true, how do we put it into motion? How do we restructure our efforts to accommodate Christ's command to make disciples rather than just casual hearers? That's next.

**That's the thing about coaches.
They don't allow the team to miss the point.**

Chapter 6

MAKING A NEW FACTORY

FOR THE NEW PRODUCT

In football terms, to build a winning team, the coach must develop effective practices. In manufacturing terms, to build a new product one needs to build a new factory. After all, whatever comes off the assembly line is a function of the processes on the assembly line. BB gun factories don't build bazookas. If you want bazookas, you must build a bazooka factory. That factory must then be fitted with structures, tools, and a power source capable of running the machinery to transform the raw materials into the desired product.

To create evangelistic disciples, we need an evangelistic discipleship factory. This factory must be powered by discipleship dynamics to enlighten and energize the work. These dynamics would deal with attitudes like getting real, making real achievements and voluntary accountability. The process of learning would be like the assembly line. It must be fitted with new discipleship structures to achieve the new end product. These classroom structures activities include discussion groups, memory verse work, study times, and times to practice communicating what was learned. Finally, the factory must be fitted with new discipleship tools to complete the new tasks required. Real progress always requires tools. Tools help people make progress together. The tools provided for this factory include memory verse cards, progress charts and even a test to help people see if they actually learned what they set out to learn. After all, the goal is not to only hear information. That could be done quickly and easily. The goal is to learn the information well enough so that the team can share it confidently and compassionately with others.

The next three chapters describe these dynamics, structures, and tools in detail. They will explain their benefits and provide practical direction for implementing each. You will also see how the leader's manuals and lesson plans create activities for these dynamics to emerge. Like a factory has many parts that fit together to create the desired end product, these new dynamics, structures and tools fit together to do the same.

Now that you have the overview of this new discipleship factory, let's tour through it one part at a time. We will begin by looking at the new power source – discipleship dynamics.

The goal is to learn the information well enough so that the team can share it confidently and compassionately with others.

Chapter 7

DISCIPLESHIP DYNAMICS

TO ENLIGHTEN AND ENERGIZE THE EFFORT

Discipleship dynamics are the power sources that provide the light of spiritual insight for the workers. When people see properly, they respond properly to their surroundings. Proper insight creates new mindsets to accompany new efforts. These dynamics are the invisible forces in the heart and spirit that produce action and change. As electricity puts metal into motion, the spiritual power in these dynamics motivates people into motion. Finally, these dynamics not only affect the individual, they create a positive chemistry within the team. Negative dynamics between people and the Lord are like grains of sand in the machinery. A positive dynamic is like oil. It lubricates the parts and frees them for smooth motion.

Would you like this kind of spiritual light, inner power and positive chemistry working in your evangelistic team? Read on. You will discover eight discipleship dynamics to empower your new factory.

Discipleship Dynamic #1
GETTING REAL

God opposes the proud but gives grace to the humble. James 4:6

Getting real is the courageous work of allowing the team to know who we really are rather than what we want to appear to be. We take off the mask of pretentious perfection and admit that we have not arrived, we acknowledge that we need practice, and we will probably make mistakes and drop the ball while we practice.

Getting real includes accurately identifying where we are. It is the willingness to say, "This is not necessarily where I want to be but it is where I am." This is the first step to getting to where the Lord wants us to be. After all, who can give us accurate direction if we don't give our accurate starting point? We must recognize and communicate the present location of our heart if we desire to make progress from there. Here are some examples: Why would anyone attempt to become more obedient to Christ if they are not willing to face the fact that they are at times disobedient to Him? Who endeavors to learn more of the Gospel if they never dare admit that they don't know enough about it to capably lead others to Christ? Would people ever pray for courage with each other if they did not confess that they are sometimes afraid? How will we ever get to the place where we love lost people more than our personal pleasures and material belongings if we don't get real enough with God and others to recognize it and admit the problem? Why work on our mental ability, verbal skills, spiritual strength and our character if we do not dare admit our deficiencies in these areas? In other words, why ask for directions if we don't admit we need them?

The *Fishers of Men* Discipleship Ministry was given birth in an atmosphere where people dared to "get real" with God and each other. I was the pastor of a small church in Linton, Indiana. It was the early months of 2007 and I had just finished a three-week series on personal evangelism. To be honest, I had a gut feeling that the messages didn't even make a dent. The church was made up of stable, mature Christians, most of whom had attended for many years. They were committed to the church and each other. The problem was the church did not grow. Neither our programs nor our people were attracting the lost and successfully connecting them to the congregation.

I was fairly new to the church and at the end of my evangelistic series, I wanted to know something. It was a little awkward to ask so I asked the congregation to bow their heads and close their eyes. They complied.

"How many of you have led someone to the Lord and helped them grow in their faith?" I asked.

Out of the 135 people present, four or five raised their hands. These were not new Christians. Most of the congregation was over fifty years old. Let me "get real" with you for a moment: I was sickened. I was frustrated and embarrassed and sought the Lord for several days.

Thanks be to God! The Lord answered me with insight completely outside my way of thinking. Here is what He spoke to my heart:

"Well, if you really want to know, you are part of the problem. You (and other pastors) are like a man who gives a few talks on football and then expects the team to play. You have no strength training, no development of fundamental skills and no practice. If a group of people competed with another team like that in football, they would be sorely beaten. Yet you will send them out against powers of darkness with no preparation. Though no one likes to admit it, their outcome is the same. They are not properly prepared."

"Furthermore, He continued, "you expect them to stay focused on outreach and they have no leadership that focuses on outreach. All they have is teaching that addresses something different almost every week."

"And lastly, you criticize the public school system for graduating kids who can't read their diploma. However, the only organization worse is my church! You don't know if my people really learned. All they have to do is listen to you talk. If they say, 'Amen! Good sermon, Preacher!' and come back next week, it is good enough. That kind of ministry and mindset has produced what we have today: people continually going to church but never being strengthened and trained to reach the lost."

I confess – His answer stung a bit. But, I knew He was right. His words gave me a whole new conviction and direction. I realized that I must go beyond preaching and teaching: I must mentor, coach and engage in discipleship. It didn't matter if I did not feel comfortable about it. God never said, "Go preach sermons and make church attenders." He said, "Go make disciples."

Soon after this revelation, I invited everyone interested to meet and talk about this matter together. Fifteen people showed up. After sharing with them what the Lord spoke to me, I told them I would like a group discussion based on this question:

> "How do you feel when you think of yourself leading others to Christ and helping them grow in their faith?"

By looking at body language and faces, it was obvious people felt awkward. Unlike Sunday's question, this time everyone's eyes were open.

People were thoughtful but no one was responding. After a minute or so, I added,

"I am not looking for the "right answer" or the victory verse: I want to know how you really feel – even if it's not pretty."

> **" I want to know how you really feel – even if it is 'not pretty.'"**

Still, the silence was deafening.

"By the way," I added, "while you are collecting your thoughts and deciding if you really want to share them, let's not try to correct anyone's comments. Let's not give some quick fix cliché answer or tell them they shouldn't feel that way. That will just shut people down and we won't get out our real feelings."

Several nodded in agreement.

Finally someone shared.

"I just don't know what to say," one said.

"Thank you," I responded, "I've been there. Anyone else ever feel that way?"

Heads nodded.

"I get started trying to explain something and then I get nervous and sometimes 'tongue-tied' and I feel like a fool," another admitted.

"I've done that too!" someone else blurted out.

I chuckled and told of a time that happened to me.

Within a few minutes, the dam broke. The barriers keeping people quiet came down and we talked openly and honestly for over an hour on the topic. It was awesome! After that we organized our thoughts and began to plot out a course for progress. Rather than feeling like we were on our endless religious treadmill going nowhere, we gained a clear sense of where we were, and where the Lord wanted us to be. Over the next several days of prayer and processing the information, the Lord helped me plot out a step-by-step plan of action for progress towards God's goal. It was exciting!

Not only was the new sense of direction exciting, the new sense of relational bonding was refreshing. This group had attended church together for many years. Now they knew each other at a much deeper level. They "got real." They found out how much they had in common deep in their heart. Several times during the conversation people said, "I thought I was the only one who every felt that way."

When the group felt safe enough to show their real selves, it was nothing short of miraculously freeing! We experienced a spiritual reality that before was only a doctrinal truth to some. James spoke of this experience this way:

"God opposes the proud but gives grace to the humble." *James 4:6*

As we let go of the pride that made us hide behind pretentious masks, we received grace from God. His presence was noticeable. His Spirit encouraged our hearts. He motivated us and gave us hope and direction for our upcoming days.

As we humbled ourselves, we also received grace from one another. Everyone knows how pride, pretentiousness, and phoniness separates people relationally. Humility healed that negative dynamic. The group became very supportive of each other. A new relational chemistry emerged. This turned out to be much more than a wonderful experience together: It was like jet fuel to our engine for the journey ahead.

Now you know why "Getting Real" is the first discipleship dynamic described. It was the first one we discovered when developing the *Fishers of Men* series. It also was the doorway to discovering many more.

As you can see, there are many benefits to instilling the discipleship dynamic of "Getting Real." It helps people locate where they really are with God and their present status quo as a fisher of men. As people dare to take off their masks and humbly show themselves for who they are, they will receive grace from God. They will also receive grace from people. Humility creates heart-to-heart bonding. Finally, getting real with God and each other creates a great atmosphere for authentic growth. Instead of being stressed by pretending to have it all together, we can admit we don't and work on getting there together.

"Getting Real" also works like oil in the machinery when we witness to others. If we are real, they are more likely to be real.

> **If we are real, they are more likely to be real.**

As a leader there are many things you can do to encourage this dynamic in your group. First, you must personally desire this dynamic. Then, you must make time for it. Third, you must model it. Fourth, create a safe atmosphere in which people can open up. The *Fishers of Men* workbooks provide a list of small group core values for the group to agree upon. These core values will help to create the safe atmosphere of order and trust.

Discipleship Dynamic #2

INCREMENTAL ACHIEVEMENT

> Therefore, since we are surrounded by such a great cloud of witnesses, let us throw off everything that hinders and the sin that so easily entangles, and let us run with perseverance the race marked out for us. *Hebrews 12:1*

Incremental Achievement is the concept of breaking down a large project into do-able parts. This proverb says it well: "How do you eat an elephant? – A bite at a time!" This dynamic is looking at the journey and realizing that the destination cannot be reached in one large step. Instead, many small steps must be mapped out. Someone once said, "Yard by yard, life is hard. Inch by inch life is a cinch!" When Jesus called His disciples, they did not immediately become fishers of men. They first followed Him. They watched. They learned. They went through life together. As they learned, they became more actively involved. When their training was complete and the time was right, the Lord empowered them with His promised Holy Spirit and sent them out to be His witnesses.

The Lord has the same plan for us. He wants us to achieve the knowledge, skills, character qualities, and spiritual power required for the work. It does not happen all at once. However, we can make step-by-step progress. All we need is for someone to guide us.

> **How do you eat an elephant?**
> **A bite at a time.**

Once people experience it, they will love the dynamic of incremental achievement. It gives hope for personal attainment. It gives them a plan that is do-able. They have a course marked out for them and they are continually passing markers along the path. They have a clear sense of direction. They know they are on the right path. They are not lost without a clue how to reach their destination. People finally feel like they are getting somewhere! Once they get a few achievements under their belt, it builds confidence, enthusiasm, and spiritual momentum for more. It brings godly fulfillment and a sense of accomplishment. They sense the Lord's smile and know that He is saying, "Well done, good and faithful servant." Money cannot buy that.

The dynamic of incremental achievement enables people to say, "Let's run the race marked out for us!" (Hebrews 12:1)

Leaders can employ this discipleship dynamic by communicating clear goals and then stating step-by-step objectives to reach the goal. From there they must give attention to accomplishing each objective. Here are two areas where the *Fishers of Men* curriculum differs from other teaching curriculums. First, the goal and objectives are laid out clearly for all to understand. Second, the lesson plan includes classroom activities to accomplish the objectives. Such activities include memorizing key scriptures, studying and reviewing key points and practicing sharing the information together. In other words, the curriculum conditions students to be doers of the Word - not just hearers. How? They do it in class together in small groups of two. In a very real sense, these manuals are not just teaching manuals; they are coaching manuals. They lay out learning times and practice times. The pace of covering information is much slower. However, the pace of actually learning information and achieving objectives is much higher.

Incremental achievement is not an individual effort in the *Fishers of Men* model. It is a group effort. It takes place within the third discipleship dynamic called Small Group Interaction.

Chapter 7   Discipleship Dynamics

Discipleship Dynamic #3
SMALL GROUP INTERACTION

> Then those who feared the LORD talked with each other, and the LORD listened and heard. A scroll of remembrance was written in his presence concerning those who feared the LORD and honored his name. *Malachi 3:16*

Small group interaction is a face-to-face encounter where those who fear the Lord talk with each other about what He says. This takes place in almost every *Fishers of Men* session. In order to accomplish this, the large group divides and spreads out throughout the room into several small groups of two. Then, using their workbooks as a guide, the small groups read Scripture and answer discussion questions together. The first questions are designed to guide them into a deeper of understanding of the verse. The latter discussion questions are aimed at helping them rightly respond to God's Word.

Small group interaction provides many positive benefits.

1. Everyone becomes 100% involved in the topic at hand. This involvement causes the interest and energy level to rise significantly.

2. Everyone – not just a few – has opportunity to share their thoughts.

3. Everyone is listened to. This itself has a powerful effect of affirming people in their faith. After all, taking interest in what someone thinks about God silently encourages them to share their thoughts with others.

> **Everyone becomes 100% involved in the topic at hand.**

4. Shy people are willing to open up in the smaller group.
5. People get to know each other and enjoy one another more.

6. Instead of hearing only the teacher share Scripture and their thoughts – they hear themselves speak God's Word and hear their responses to it. This creates a deeper level of spiritual formation of convictions and personal ownership.

7. The topic becomes more personal and meaningful.

8. As people become comfortable talking about God with one another inside the church, they will become more comfortable sharing their faith with others outside the church.

9. As people get to know each other better, they start to care for each other more. This increased capacity to care for others is just as important as the increased capacity to understand and discuss God's Word.

10. Last, but certainly not least, God listens to the conversations. Malachi 3:16 reveals that He is honored when we talk to each other about what He is saying to us.

Given all these benefits of small group interaction, we can see that sometimes people do not need to hear *the teacher* say the Word of God: they need to hear *themselves* say the Word of God. His Word needs to be in *their* mouth. Small group interaction provides that opportunity in a safe and controlled atmosphere.

The leader plays an important role in facilitating this dynamic. As you follow the lesson plan, it will provide the time and the direction for small group interaction. Make sure everyone understands the directions before starting.

Encourage the group to share the leadership responsibilities during discussion times. One person will lead the conversation for workbook question one. The other person should lead the conversation for question two. From there they should continually alternate. After all, one of the key goals of relational evangelism preparation is to help each other get comfortable leading and initiating conversations.

As the leader, you will have to manage the time. Let the group know the time limits they have to work with so they can pace themselves accordingly.

Manage your time as best you can as you endeavor to follow the leading of the Holy Spirit and meet the needs of the group. Sometimes learning and processing information does not fit in our nice neat time slots. Rather than rushing through the session or skipping vital learning activities, draw a line in the lesson where you left off and start there next time.

Join a small group yourself once direction is given and needs are met. This shows the groups that you enjoy learning with them. Your example will encourage others. Let them know that you desire to operate as a co-leader and co-learner in the group. Therefore, you want your partner to take the initiative in leading the conversation in half of the question.

If your class seems to need your attention during an activity, make yourself available to help others rather than joining a small group. Take the time also to observe how well people are interacting. Confirm that they are working according to the directions given and are relating in a way that respects the small group core values. You may even join in on a conversation for one question and then continue to wander to other places in the room.

One thing is for sure: you and those you lead are going to enjoy small group interaction. They are also going to be prepared, encouraged and built up from it in ways that many have never before experienced.

Discipleship Dynamic #4
VOLUNTARY ACCOUNTABILITY

> Submit to one another out of reverence for Christ. *Ephesians 5:21*
>
> Be diligent in these matters; give yourself wholly to them, so that everyone may see your progress. *1 Timothy 4:15*

The *Fishers of Men* style of accountability differs in several ways from the authoritarian style that takes place in our legal system, workplace, and between children and parents. First, it is voluntary rather than forced. Second, this accountability deals with only the scope of cooperating together to achieve specific goals and objectives in the classroom. It is not the cult-like manipulation of a leader micro-managing other people's lives. Thirdly, this dynamic is mutual among everyone. People make themselves accountable to each other in small groups of two while working on projects. Even the group leader voluntarily gives account for his learning and newly acquired skills. Thus, voluntary accountability simply means people give others permission to help them, learn with them, and become accountability partners who verify each other's progress. It happens very naturally throughout the structured learning activities described in the next chapter.

The small group system allows for this dynamic without putting the leader in the position of having to coach everyone. Many leaders, myself included, would feel overwhelmed trying to give personal attention to everyone's personal progress. This system puts everyone in the position of playing the role of coach and player on an alternating basis. One moment you will be checking a person's progress; the next moment they will be checking yours. The activities in the workbook provide the direction for these times.

The benefits of implementing voluntary accountability between partners and the leader are many. It helps people get beyond mere talk and engage in real action. It helps everyone stay focused and take their progress seriously.

Voluntary accountability gets people caring about each other's progress. The attention of others makes our progress matter more and therefore inspires

Chapter 7   Discipleship Dynamics

more effort. Finally, as Ephesians 5:21 and 1 Timothy 4:15 state, following Christ together with this kind of submission to one another for the purpose of obeying Christ creates real progress. It also allows us and our partners the ability to see our progress.

As a leader, you can encourage this dynamic in many ways. Show them what this dynamic is and what it is not. It is not one person trying to be in control over others. It is submitting to one another for the sake of becoming bigger, stronger and better for our Lord. Let the group know that you will be voluntarily accountable to small group partners also. You will check their progress and they will check yours. Show them the benefits that all will receive. Encourage them to openly invite the process and to appreciate their partners who provide voluntary accountability.

When you see people helping each other achieve new skills, you will be glad you discovered this discipleship dynamic!

Discipleship Dynamic #5
INTENTIONAL SHARING

> *For what I received, I passed on to you as of first importance: that Christ died for our sins according to the Scriptures.*
> *1 Corinthians 15:3*

The dynamic of Intentional Sharing is faithfully and deliberately passing on what we receive to others. The Apostle Paul describes this dynamic "as of first importance." In other words, he knew that God expected him to.

Intentional Sharing develops hearts to share with anyone we can. It may be our children or our family members. It may be a friend, a neighbor or a co-worker – a Christian or a non-Christian. Of course, the goal is to ultimately share with people who do not know the Lord. However, this dynamic is not limited to just them. God wants everyone to hear His good news.

> **God wants everyone to hear His good news.**

Intentional sharing works to build relationships where we can share what we are learning on a regular basis. We share as much as we can without overwhelming people! As we become more skillful in our conversations, we learn how to engage others by asking questions and capturing interest. When people are included and interested, we are able to share more with them than if they are disinterested.

Developing this dynamic will bring many benefits on three levels. The students benefit personally. Those who hear the message benefit greatly. And finally, this dynamic benefits God's Kingdom. Let's briefly consider each:

1. **The students benefit personally**

Students will be inspired to think differently. Instead of mentally processing the lesson only in a way in which the information relates to them, they now add a new facet of thinking. Now they also think of how they will share the information with others. As they share with others, they remember it better themselves and process it more deeply in their heart.

Edgar Dale (April 27, 1900 – March 8, 1985) a professor of education at Ohio State University, put it this way.

"We remember

- 10% of what we hear
- 20% of what we read
- 30% of what we see
- 50% of what we see and hear
- 70% of what we discuss with others
- 80% of what we personally experience
- 95% of what we teach others."

Though these numbers are general estimates and though there are many other factors related to memory and learning, the point is this: The more we involve ourselves with what we learn, the more we learn. If we share with others what we have learned, we will remember more.

Let's make this really simple. The age-old phrase was written in negative terms but it is still true. It simply says: "Use it or lose it!" Intentional Sharing spurs people to "use it."

Here is a third practical benefit to students. The more they share God's Word, the better they get at it. Practice makes perfect.

2. The benefit others receive

When we share with others the things we have received, they receive insight, encouragement, and spiritual seed that will grow in their hearts for years to come. Those who sow seeds make far more spiritual change in the landscape of the future than they realize. Imagine if twenty-five years ago two men each had a bag of apple seeds. One tilled the soil, planted and watered his seeds; the other left his in the bag. The difference would be vast. Apples cannot even start to compare with spiritual seed. Apples and apple trees die. God's Word bears fruit in people's lives for eternity!

> **God's Word bears fruit in people's lives for eternity!**

3. The benefit to God and His Kingdom
When we share God's words with others, we honor Him. We show Him that His Word truly is important to us. We show Him that we hold His Word in our heart longer than the time it takes to leave church or our place of study. In fact, we show Him that our heart is full enough of His Word that it overflows out of our mouth. When others hear God's Word, it expands God's influence and enlarges His Kingdom.

There are several steps we can take to promote this dynamic of Intentional Sharing. First, give attention to it – especially during the later weeks in each unit when students have the information down well enough to pass it on. Put on this completely new mindset: You are not just giving out information for your students to *know*. You are preparing your students so that they have awesome information to *share!* You are not just teaching. You are coaching. You are equipping, encouraging, and motivating the team to become wise, loving, confident voices for our Lord in their area of influence. You are working for this outcome at the end of each unit:

> By the end of each unit each student knows the information well enough that they will easily share it with others from their head and their heart.

Imagine this. If you have a group of twelve, by the end of the eight-week unit, twelve other people are going to hear at least some of the things you have been learning together. If people capture this dynamic of intentional sharing, you will multiply your efforts many times over through them. Over the years, each of you will share with many others. This dynamic works to get the seed of God's Word out of the bags and scattered in the fields! There it will produce eternal fruit.

Here is another thing to work on as a leader. Help your team deal with the fear of failure. Many people are afraid of sharing their faith because they worry that they won't be very good at it. The truth is, they may be right – at first. Who never falls while learning to ride a bike? The issue is not if people will stumble along the way: The issue is what will they do when they stumble? Encourage them to just get back up and try again. Their tenth attempt will be far better than their first. So, rather than being paralyzed by the fear of failure, let's help them hurry and get to the tenth time! Let's get out there and make some mistakes! After all, the biggest mistake is to let fear paralyze us. We shouldn't take our egos so seriously. We could take a lot of pressure off ourselves if we humbly admitted that we are not theologians. We don't have all the answers. We may not say it all perfectly. Nevertheless, we are willing to share what we are learning. It is not about us. It is about Jesus.

Preparing people to pass on what they learn is an exciting challenge. Many will come to Christ as their Lord and Savior because you allowed God to use you to get people ready to pass it on!

Stop for a moment. Sit back and imagine what will take place in the days and years ahead if you impart the discipleship dynamic of Intentional Sharing to a team of people. Let the picture develop in your mind. Believe God for it. I guarantee that He desires you to succeed in this effort. It's a no brainer. It is certainly His will so you can confidently ask Him for help with the effort. Let this concept germinate and take root in you. You will be glad you did.

Speaking of being glad – that brings us to Discipleship Dynamic #6. It is called "Celebration of Progress."

Discipleship Dynamic #6
CELEBRATION OF PROGRESS

> His master replied, "Well done, good and faithful servant! You have been faithful with a few things; I will put you in charge of many things. Come and share your master's happiness!"
> *Matthew 25:21*

Celebration of Progress is following Jesus' example to recognize and honor accomplishments. It gives attention to work well done. It is sharing in the Lord's happiness for His servants' faithfulness and resulting achievement.

> **Celebration of progress is following Jesus' example.**

This dynamic creates a positive culture of mutual appreciation and respect for work well done. This kind of attention adds life to the person, the team and the task at hand. Too many times people get fooled into thinking about only what is wrong in their life and the life of others. Then, they completely miss all the things that are right. What a drudgery. Why is it a drudgery? Whether we like to admit it or not, people need attention. It is like fuel for their inner engine. People thrive on positive attention. People need to be needed. They need to be appreciated. When their efforts and progress are recognized, they are inspired to do more. Why? Because they now realize that what they do *matters*. When something matters, people are willing to commit to it and sacrifice for it.

Here are steps you can take to encourage this dynamic in your group, your family and others.

1. Talk about this dynamic during teachable moments.
2. Lead your team to make recognizable progress.
3. When they make progress, take time to express happiness with them.

4. Be enthusiastic about the journey.
5. Let them sense the Lord's joy over their faithfulness.
6. Help your team celebrate each other's progress. Ask them to reflect on what they appreciate about their partners and what progress they see them making.

My friend, stop and think. Let this soak in. God is watching your progress – even right now. He is happy about it! Take a moment to be happy with Him. Then, think about the efforts and progress you see in those around you. Tell them about it and show your appreciation. Finally, watch the difference it makes when you celebrate their progress.

Discipleship Dynamic #7
CLEAR VISION FOR CONTINUOUS PROGRESS

Then the LORD replied: "Write down the revelation and make it plain on tablets so that a herald may run with it." *Habakkuk 2:2*

Clear vision is seeing the big picture. It understands what the end product looks like. It knows how it is supposed to work and what to do so that it does. When people get God's clear vision for becoming fishers of men, they can then "run with it." That is, they can make continued progress.

Here is the challenge: Continued *progress* requires continued *work*. Many people today only want those things which are "quick and easy." Products and services claiming to quickly solve problems with little effort or investment, are an easy sell. However, if someone says the solution will take time, effort and investment many will give up before they start.

Can you imagine what it would have been like if the disciples had this mindset? Imagine them asking Jesus if following Him would be quick and easy? What if they asked, "How many weeks will your discipleship program require?" Imagine the Lord's response if they gave the following suggestions to accommodate their mindset:

"Perhaps a three week mini-series would work best."

"People are too busy for long-term commitments."

"Don't spend more than forty-five minutes in a session."

"Whatever you do, don't expect people to really learn what you say and certainly don't quiz or test them on it; they will not come to your classes."

How do you suppose that would that go over with the eternal Lord of heaven and earth?

This may sound odd at first, but I think Jesus might have told them a story like our modern-day fable titled, "The Three Little Pigs." Its lesson is clear: Brick houses are not built with straw house commitments. Straw houses may go up quickly, easily and with little personal investment, but in the end, they are not worth anything either. One wolf or another will easily blow them down. Brick houses cost more, and require more time and effort. However, they are far stronger and last far longer.

> # **Brick houses are not built with straw house commitments.**

If Jesus were in the story, He would have been the brick salesman. The wolf would have also masqueraded as the sticks and straw salesman. Why? He knew he could blow those down. There is a spiritual lesson there. Perhaps we should be suspicious of the concept of "quick and easy" – especially when building our lives and things for eternity.

Now let's look at what the Apostle Paul wrote in Scripture about this matter. God expects quality work from his people. He not only expects quality work - He will test it. Look how the Apostle Paul says that God will test our ministry of teaching, evangelism and discipleship:

> By the grace God has given me, I laid a foundation as an expert builder, and someone else is building on it. But each one should be careful how he builds. [11] For no one can lay any foundation other than the one already laid, which is Jesus Christ. [12] If any man builds on this foundation using gold, silver, costly stones, wood, hay or straw, [13] his work will be shown for what it is, because the Day will bring it to light. It will be revealed with fire, and the fire will test the quality of each man's work. [14] If what he has built survives, he will receive his reward. [15] If it is burned up, he will suffer loss; he himself will be saved, but only as one escaping through the flames.
> *I Corinthians 3:10 - 15*

Wow! That's a wake-up call. God expects quality work from his people. He not only expects quality work, He will test it.

I want to pass His test. Therefore, even if some people want the quick and easy approach, I am not building with wood, hay or straw. I am selling only quality products with quality workmanship. Furthermore, I want to help others so that their efforts also pass His test. Following Jesus and being discipled and trained is not quick. It is not necessarily easy either. It requires stretching, effort and practice.

The *Fishers of Men* Series is not a quick fix. It is relational discipleship. It will require more time and commitment than a straw house. It is a brick house. All that said, we must be flexible enough to that people can stay involved with it. Here are some practical helps to assist you and your team.

1. To help people (and perhaps yourself) make continued progress over the discipleship journey, make the attendance requirements flexible for those who are occasionally absent due to work, vacation and emergencies. With their workbooks, they can complete the objectives at home, on line, or out-of-town. They can get with a partner on the phone and keep up with everyone else. Think of it as a college course with alternative on-line classes for make–up when needed. This will make the effort far more doable.

2. Change class locations occasionally for new scenery.

3. Enlist others to help you. Let them assist with preparations, promotion, phone calling and organizing.

4. Finally, let others help lead some of the classes or even some of the units. It will give you a break, allow you to be a student, and allow them the opportunity to practice their leadership. Allowing others to help you will allow you the ability to keep a clear focus on the vision and to help others make continued progress.

Stop for a moment. Focus in on this clear vision:

> Years from now when you look back on your life, you will value the quality investments you made in other lives for the Lord. You will experience a satisfaction far richer than that which would come from the short term, temporary pursuits that lead to nowhere. Keep that in mind. Let it motivate you to press for continued progress.

Discipleship Dynamic # 8
COURAGE TO TAKE NEW STEPS

> Be strong and courageous, because you will lead these people to inherit the land I swore to their forefathers to give them. *Joshua 1:6*

Courage is the willingness to step out of one's comfort zone and into a new challenge for God. Courage faces the fear of potential loss and presses forward believing in God's promised gain. When God appointed Joshua to lead His people into His promised land, He knew it would require courage on Joshua's part. Wicked giants awaited his arrival and were more than willing to provide the loss. Moving forward required large inner resources of faith in God and personal courage.

Courage to take new steps is a vital dynamic in this discipleship process. It takes courage to get real with God and others. It takes nerve to face the fear of failure and take steps of incremental achievement. Shy people must dare to participate in small group interaction and pray with others. Voluntary accountability requires a humble and courageous resolve to overcome the potential dread of someone else looking at their performance. In the same token, it may require obedient nerve to be that "someone else" who confirms the progress of a partner. Intentionally sharing with others certainly requires courage for some. Pressing on to make continued progress in the face of all life's temporary urgencies requires brick-like commitment and courage. The only dynamic that does not require courage is the celebration of progress. However, without courage there will not be much of that either.

Discipleship requires courage.

These dynamics and the courage required to achieve them mark the distinct differences between those who merely go to church and hear sermons and those intent on becoming disciples. Discipleship requires far more commitment and courage!

God prepared Joshua for a physical battle. Our battle today is a different kind of battle than in Joshua's day:

> For our struggle is not against flesh and blood, but against the rulers, against the authorities, against the powers of this dark world and against the spiritual forces of evil in the heavenly realms. *Ephesians 6:12*

We are not called to kill those who oppose us. We are called to overcome spiritual forces of evil. Wrong spirits inspire wrong thoughts, wrong words and wrong actions. We all know how to contend with flesh. Swords, guns, bullets and bombs handle that rather nicely. However, spiritual battles require spiritual weapons.

> The weapons we fight with are not the weapons of the world. On the contrary, they have divine power to demolish strongholds. ⁵We demolish arguments and every pretension that sets itself up against the knowledge of God, and we take captive every thought to make it obedient to Christ. *1 Corinthians 10:4 -5*

Our weapons are spiritual. They have God's divine power to destroy opposing spiritual strongholds. Those strongholds reveal themselves in arguments, attitudes, pretentions and thoughts that exalt themselves against God. Think about it this way. Everything that people say and do is really just the web. The inner spirit inspiring the work is the spider. Spiritual warfare goes after the spider! The goal is not just to kill the inner spiritual spider. The goal is to replace the spider with a new inhabitant - the Holy Spirit of God. He inspires obedience to Christ.

That's the battle we are called to fight. Our sword is not metal. Our sword is our tongue. It is our words. Metal cuts only flesh. Words can change hearts. We need not rely on our words for this task. We are to use God's Word.

Here is another mystery behind this battle: God chooses to use His people to overcome powers of darkness rather than doing it all Himself. When Satan attacked man with deception in the Garden of Eden (Genesis 3:1), God declared that one day the seed of a woman – a man – would attack Satan. Satan might strike his heel but man would crush his head! (Genesis 3:15) Christ fulfilled God's declaration when He defeated Satan's curse on the cross. However, God still includes His children in the battle and the victory over the devil. His Word says:

> The God of peace will soon crush Satan under your feet. *Romans 16:20*

That's awesome. Look at your feet right now. God is going to crush Satan under them! No. Your goodness and power alone will not accomplish that feat. God does most of the work. He first sent His Son to save you from the curse of sin. Then He restores you, equips you, and empowers you with His Spirit. Then He says to the devil, "You messed with my children! Now my children are going to mess with you!"

Can you hear it? I hear "Rocky *" music playing in the background! It is playing for you!

Can you hear it? I hear "Rocky" music playing in the background!

The fact is, God could have easily taken Satan out on His own right then. However, that was not His plan. God wants the greater satisfaction to see His children do the job with His power in them. That's why God chooses to use us rather than do it Himself. Furthermore, this way requires faith, obedience and courage on our part. Faith in God and courage for God honors God. Dear friends, let that inspire you to have courage!

Once we understand God's plan to crush Satan under our feet, we begin to see things differently. We are not idle bystanders. We no longer ask for God alone to overcome Satan. We put on God's armor and take our stand against him! We wait expectantly for the day God crushes him under our feet!

---

* "Rocky" (1976) is an academy award-winning movie starring Sylvester Stallone as an obscure Philadelphia boxer who gets his dream shot to become the heavyweight champion. This rousing drama (and music) inspired audiences around the world. Director: John G Avidsen   Rated PG

And, while we are waiting, let's get in spiritual shape, gain skill with God's sword, courageously follow the Lord's leading and do our best for Him.

Courage to Take New Steps is a power discipleship dynamic. Here are some steps you can take to encourage this dynamic among those you lead:

1. Realize that God calls you to be strong and courageous yourself.
2. Pray for your group.
3. Encourage them with these insights.
4. Fellowship with strong and courageous people.

Chapter 7   Discipleship Dynamics

Reflections on
DISCIPLESHIP DYNAMICS

When activated, these discipleship dynamics create a completely new spiritual chemistry between people. They relate to one another more freely. Their positive response to each other adds another life of its own. They "click" with one another. Their unity brings the power of synergy rather than the destructive forces of discord. They become stronger together than what they could have been alone. They build each other up instead of just thinking about themselves or, worse yet, tearing each other down. These discipleship dynamics create an atmosphere just like God gave His people in King Hezekiah's day.

> Also in Judah the hand of God was on the people to give them unity of mind to carry out what the king and his officials had ordered, following the word of the LORD. *2 Chronicles 30:12*

These dynamics also activate a new spiritual chemistry between people and God. When God's people begin to get real with Him and make progress together, it brings God's smile and sweet presence. This is huge! Some people have gone to church all their lives and never recognized the presence of God. People become "in tune" to His presence and His leading. As they sense Him, He gives grace and strength to take on the challenges ahead.

> For the eyes of the LORD range throughout the earth to strengthen those whose hearts are fully committed to him.
> *2 Chronicles 16:9*

As you can see, taking the time to develop powerful godly dynamics between people can be as important as teaching correct doctrine.

Perhaps you are thinking, "It looks good, but how do I make it all fit in a classroom setting?" Read on. New discipleship structures and tools were organized to do just that!

Chapter 8

DISCIPLESHIP STRUCTURES TO PROMOTE PROGRESS

Discipleship Structures are the way class time and people are organized to create an atmosphere where discipleship dynamics emerge and move the group towards the goal. The old structure of rows of chairs facing a lectern is removed. A new kind of arrangement is implemented. The old lecture and listening is also radically remodeled. New structures that promote active discipleship rather than passive listening are implemented. Let's look at these structured learning activities now in closer detail.

Structure #1
OPENING DISCUSSION GROUPS

Opening Discussion Groups are small circles of four to six people that talk about the opening discussion question together. Here is a discussion question taken from a session in Unit 1: "Committing to the Call":

"Tell your favorite fishing story. If you do not have a fishing story, share your thoughts on fishing."

This structure benefits the group in many ways. It allows everyone to share in a five-to-ten minute period. It creates 100% involvement and helps people get to know each other. Though they may not get to know the whole group, they get to know some of the group. They discover common ground and become comfortable with each other. As people engage in storytelling and sharing history, they begin to bond. In short, it's relational. Since the goal is to prepare people for relational evangelism, these groups promote relational discipleship.

> **Discussion groups promote relational discipleship.**

The second benefit of opening discussion groups is that the questions create an enjoyable atmosphere and interest in the theme for the session.

Finally, these activities prepare people's hearts to "get real" with each other. Sharing history in a light-hearted atmosphere encourages relationships and lays the groundwork for trust. When people become comfortable with each other and trust each other, it paves the way for them to relate on a deeper, more personal level.

The leader's role in creating this structure is quite simple. Once you pose the introduction question to the whole group and give the directions provided in the leader's manual, direct the students to divide into small groups of four to six people for the discussion time. Tell them to make as much space as possible between the groups. Communicate how much time is available for this activity so that they pace themselves accordingly. Finally, once direction is given, join a group so that you also reap its benefits.

After the activity, ask for a few brief highlights from the groups. Enjoy the opportunity. Finally, use the momentum gained during this time to lead into the session introduction and upcoming activities. The workbook will provide a transitional sentence for you. Make sure you understand how the discussion relates to the topic and you will make that transition with confidence and ease.

Structure #2
COOPERATIVE LEARNING GROUPS

Cooperative learning groups are the heartbeat of the *Fishers of Men* discipleship series. Small groups of two work together for the purpose of helping each other learn, gain witnessing skills and grow. They fulfill God's desire expressed in Ephesians 4:

> From him the whole body, joined and held together by every supporting ligament, grows and builds itself up in love, as each part does its work. *Ephesians 4:16*

"Cooperative Learning Groups" are usually referred to as simply "Small Groups" in the workbooks. It sounds less technical. However, as the groups understand *cooperative* learning, they will know how to relate to each other and reap the benefits.

Cooperative Learning Groups engage in the following three basic activities:

1. Scripture reading and discussion
2. Personal Coaching Time
3. Small group prayer

Let's look at each in more detail.

Small Group Activity #1: Scripture reading and discussion.

The student's workbooks provide the Scriptures and the discussion questions. These questions help students understand the Scripture and apply it to their lives. The questions also help the students probe their hearts and get to

> **Cooperative learning groups are the heartbeat of this ministry.**

know each other better.

Doing this activity in small groups rather than the large group provides many benefits. First of all, it is enjoyable. Everyone gets involved. Shy people feel comfortable sharing with an audience of one. People take more ownership for the lesson. Everything becomes more personal and more relational. People start to truly know and like each other. They gain experience in putting their thoughts about God into words. They then become less fearful to share their heart. Last but not least, something happens when people talk about God and others listen. Their sense of personal significance is strengthened, their confidence increases, and they begin to realize that if their heart for God matters to people inside the church, it just may matter to others outside the church also.

Small Group Activity #2: Personal Coaching Time

Personal Coaching Time takes the small group beyond discussion and helps students attain personal knowledge and scriptural skills. It includes a variety of exercises described below.

> **Students attain personal knowledge and scriptural skills.**

Personal Coaching Exercise #1: Scripture Memory Work

This exercise provides practice time for small groups to memorize a key Scripture related to the unit goal.

In many churches, Scripture memorization is only practiced by small children. They do it to get a star on a piece of paper or win a prize. However, this discipleship ministry mobilizes adults to memorize Scripture together for far greater reasons.

1. Memorizing Scripture gets God's Word into their minds.

2. Memorizing Scripture gets God's Word into their hearts.
3. When people's hearts are full of God's Word, they begin to speak about it to others.
4. Speaking God's Word is better than speaking our own words.
5. Speaking God's Word skillfully is better than speaking it unskillfully.

These are the reasons *why* we memorize God's Word together. Now let's look at *how* we memorize His Word together: In this exercise, students recite the memory verse back and forth to each other out loud. When the first person says the verse for the first time, they say it in a way that emphasizes the first word in the verse. Their partner then says the verse in a way that puts emphasis on the second word. It is not that they say the second word louder but they say the verse as though that word is the most important word in the phrase. The first person responds by reciting the verse again – putting emphasis on the third word. They continue this process until the verse has been recited with attention given to each word. Even the small words like "and" should be emphasized. Here is an example of the process. The word in bold letters is the one emphasized during that repetition.

1st person: "**Come**, follow me, Jesus said, "and I will make you fishers of men."
Matthew 4:19

2nd person: "Come, **follow** me, Jesus said, "and I will make you fishers of men."
Matthew 4:19

1st person: "Come, follow **me**, Jesus said, "and I will make you fishers of men."
Matthew 4:19

2nd person: "Come, follow me, **Jesus** said, "and I will make you fishers of men."
Matthew 4:19

Continue that pattern until the verse along with the book, chapter and verse are emphasized.

At first, some students will forget which word they are supposed to emphasize once they get a few words into the process. This tip will help them. Have them put their finger on the word being emphasized at that moment and slide it to the next word at the right time.

Once the team has said the verse enough times to emphasize every word, practice saying the verse without looking at it. If there is a second verse, begin that verse in the same fashion. For the moment, work on only the second verse. When the second phrase is complete, practice saying the two verses together without looking at the verses. Continue the process until all the verses are complete.

Make sure that the teams fix the Scripture reference in their minds as well as the text. This allows them to show the verse to others in the Bible. It also proves that they are speaking God's Word rather than their own and communicates His authority.

Memorizing this way will help your team in many ways. Looking at the verse and saying it aloud helps them to focus. People see and hear the verse many times. Repetition of effort brings success. Every word receives attention and provides insight to the whole verse. Students gain the practice of quoting God's word to someone else. It is one thing to think we know a Scripture. It is another thing to confidently quote it to others. Finally, this process helps students gain personal skill with God's Word in a relatively short time.

Here is another benefit. Students can begin to engage in discipleship dynamics during this exercise as you share them. Everyone has an occasion to *"get real"* with their memory verse partner. Pride and pretenses of perfection can't hide in this activity. People will make mistakes, get mental blocks, and be humbled by the fact that they occasionally "drop the ball" during this practice. Some patience is required. The fear of failure must be faced head-on. Some laughter (at ourselves, not others) is helpful and relieves stress. God gives grace to the humble. The dynamic of *incremental achievement* also becomes a reality in this exercise. People learn word-by-word, phrase-by-phrase and verse-by-verse. They are not just hearing the verse: They are achieving the personal ability to share it themselves. *Small group interaction* and *voluntary accountability* take place naturally as people learn out loud together. There is no better way to prepare to *intentionally share* God's Word than to share it with a partner in class. They make *continued progress* together as they exercise their *courage to take this new step*. Finally, when the team memorizes their verse, they have a legitimate occasion to *celebrate progress*. Notice how the discipleship dynamics (highlighted in italics) give life and purpose to the activity. Notice also how the activity provides an occasion for the dynamics to become reality in relationships. This is interactive, experiential discipleship in action!

As the leader, do your best to join in a small group. Rather than learning the verse in advance, let someone help you learn it just as everyone else is doing. They need to see you practice what you preach about getting real, voluntary accountability and every other dynamic described. If they see you make a mistake and try again, they will feel more comfortable when they make a mistake.

Once you and your team memorize the verse, make sure you celebrate the moment! If the joy of achievement is greater than the stress of the effort, the team will press on to continue achieving more for the Lord.

Personal Coaching Exercise #2: Review Key Information

This exercise leads students to rehearse key information from previous lessons before learning new material. The workbook provides direction and review questions.

The reasons for this exercise are obvious: Most of our memories and spiritual comprehension are not as good as we like to admit. Jesus explained the matter this way in the parable of the sower:

> "A farmer went out to sow his seed. ⁴As he was scattering the seed, some fell along the path, and the birds came and ate it up." *Matthew 13:4*

> "Listen then to what the parable of the sower means: ¹⁹When anyone hears the message about the kingdom and does not understand it, the evil one comes and snatches away what was sown in his heart. This is the seed sown along the path." *Matthew 13:18-19*

If the Lord's words are not understood well, they are like listening to someone talk and all we hear is "Bla... bla... bla..." Those words are not remembered long. Jesus said the evil one (Satan) comes like a flock of birds and snatches them away. Stolen seed doesn't help anyone. Hearing it once only to have it gone later is a waste of effort.

Reviewing key information helps students retain God's Word. It transfers information from our shallow, short-term memory deeper into our long-term memory.

This discipline of review also deepens our understanding. The second look almost always provides new insights. It is like watching a movie or reading a book a second time. There are always things there that were not recognized the first time. Along with that, a word or a thought becomes more emphatic. The inner light bulb comes on. What was once a monotone noise now has deep meaning.

In order to take the time to review key information, we must care about the information. If the seed is not important enough to move to soft soil and be buried and watered, it will not last long. If the seed is cared for it will remain, sprout, produce fruit and feed others.

The desired outcome for each *Fishers of Men* unit is to prepare students to know the information well enough so that each person can share it with others from their head and their heart. To accomplish this outcome, a consistent practice of review is required. After all, we can only share what we understand. We can only share what we remember. We can only share what is presently occupying and overflowing from our heart.

Ask your students to answer the review questions from memory before reviewing their notes. This will provide a better mental exercise – even if it is not pretty. After all, the goal is to exercise their memory and personal understanding – even if the exercise creates a little stress. Once they try to recall the information without looking, they may refer to their notes to make sure they remembered correctly.

It might be tempting to skip review for the sake of time – until you imagine the hungry birds flocking overhead. Their presence motivates us to properly bury the new seed. Quality long-term results are better than quick short-term progress.

Personal Coaching Exercise #3: Communication Practice

Communication practice is closely related to reviewing. Reviewing key information helps to assure that students retain key information. Communication practice helps to assure that students can share the information with others. After all, it is one thing to have salt in our shaker: it is another thing to get it out. The more comfortable people become in sharing information, the more likely they are to share it. Let's face it. Most Christians hear much but share little. We need a little shaking to get His Word out of us to others. This exercise does that.

Communication practice is included at the end of many small group discussions. It is not identified as "Communication Practice." The workbook directions simply state, "Practice sharing this point with each other as though you were sharing it with a friend."

Personal Coaching Exercise #4: Pursuing the Unit Goal and Objectives

Pursuing the Unit Goal and Objectives is the practice of reviewing objectives, accomplishing the objectives, showing a partner the accomplishment and having them check off the objective in the workbook when it is completed. Each partner does this for the other.

Unit objectives are divided into three basic categories – Learning Objectives, Personal Growth Objectives and Specific Action Objectives.

1. Learning Objectives relate to specific mastery of God's Word or key points in the unit. One example of a learning objective is learning assigned memory verses. As the students work on the memory verse together, they are pursuing one of the unit objectives.

2. Personal Growth Objectives relate to our inner person - our confidence, our compassion or our character. Though measuring these are much more subjective, they are valid objectives and they help the students intentionally work to grow in these areas.

3. Specific Action Objectives include a few important requirements that relate to achieving the unit goal. They may range from simple tasks such

Chapter 8 Discipleship Structures to Promote Progress

as using the discipleship tools to sharing the essence of what was learned with a non-believer.

Personal Coaching Exercise #5: Study for the Unit Test

Study for the unit test is often one in the same as reviewing key information. In many cases the review questions are taken right from the unit test so they are accomplishing both in one effort. The unit test, with an answer page, is located in the student's manual so it is convenient to review together. Students know exactly what they are expected to learn. Time is provided to study for the test in class through reviews. Students may and should also study at home. More information about the test is given in the coming pages.

Most people are agitated at the thought of a test. They are afraid of them so they avoid them. We don't. In fact, we are not studying to pass only a paper test. We are studying to pass a spiritual test. The spiritual test is this: Do we know this truth well enough so that we can accurately and confidently share it with others in a way that persuades them to follow Christ? Our students should also realize that a confident knowledgeable presentation is far more effective than a timid and inaccurate presentation. That realization makes us more accountable for our personal preparation. We cannot relegate all preparation for success to prayer or God's sovereignty. We cannot blame all failure to reach people on the devil's interference or people's stubbornness. These are certainly all factors. However, our skill level, our confidence, and ability are also factors. Well-trained sales people who know their product, are enthused about their product, and can communicate clearly and confidently the benefits of their product sell more than those who don't.

Our product is Jesus. He is best product in all history. That is why we study. That is why we test ourselves to make sure we know our facts, so that we can promote the Lord in such a way that others will come to Him. Hence, we must help people get beyond the self-centered desire for ease. We must inspire them to get over their fear of failure and joyfully prepare for something eternally good! If we are going to be disciples instead of casual hearers, we must be healed of our allergies to test.

Let's briefly review the Personal Coaching Time exercises:

1. *Scripture Memory Work* exercises students' skill with God's Word.
2. *Reviewing Key Information* exercises students' personal understanding and memory.
3. *Communication Practice* enables students to say what they know.
4. *Pursuing Unit Objectives* provides direction and a clear sense of progress.
5. *Study for the Unit Test* prepares the team for capable, confident ministry.

Personal Coaching Time is a powerful concept for Cooperative Learning Groups. They create 100% involvement. Everyone engages in and takes personal ownership for their interaction with God's Word. It helps the team take steps of incremental achievement. It provides the framework for the dynamic of voluntary accountability. Everyone receives personal attention and support. Everyone realizes that their effort and progress matters to others. It helps people make progress and even provides a format to celebrate the progress made. And, as you can now see, it provides a powerful learning and growing atmosphere. Using the workbook as a guide, this structure enables teachers to talk less and allows people to grow more. And, it's enjoyable! Why haven't we thought of this before?

Don't worry about how you will remember, let alone implement, this new information. These structures are built into the lesson plan with step-by-step instructions provided. You could easily lead a *Fishers of Men* group without reading this manual. However, you will be a much better leader and motivator now that you understand the philosophy, benefits, convictions, and insights that developed the activities. When we know why we should do something, we are far more likely to do it that if we do not know why.

Small Group Activity #3: Small Group Prayer

Small group prayer takes place at the end of the session. During this activity, groups of two pray for one another in response to what the Lord is speaking to their hearts through the session. The workbook also provides suggestions for this time. After that much discussion together, students are primed and ready for prayer.

Chapter 8 Discipleship Structures to Promote Progress

Small group prayer energizes the group the same way small group discussion energizes the group. Everyone gets involved. Everyone takes personal ownership for the time. Spiritual energy erupts in the room as people begin pouring themselves out to God for each other. People pray for themselves and their partner in far deeper ways than if praying in a large group. It is immensely more personal. Finally, as they interact with the Lord in response to His Word, greater conviction, courage and compassion develops in their hearts. This team is growing mentally so that they know enough to fish for men. They are also developing spiritually so that they dare enough and care enough.

Some people will be uncomfortable with small group prayer at first. Through the years I have had more than one person approach me weeks later and say,

"You scared the life out of me by making me pray out loud with another person! I've never done that before in my life!"

I would laugh and say,

"Good! I suppose that, if we are going to learn how to pray for lost people to come to know Christ, we had better start practicing by praying for each other here. Glad to see you conquered the challenge!"

Approaching God in prayer is like anything else in life: It gets better with practice. As people learn how to approach God together in the group, they will become ready to pray with others outside the group.

Does this get you excited? It does me. Honestly, I think the Lord gets excited over it too. I can almost hear Him saying, "Finally, My people being equipped, trained and discipled rather than just talked to! Finally, My people are going to grow in skills instead of just go to church! Finally, My people are not going to hear the preacher talk one more time – *they* are going to learn how to talk about Me!"

I love it when I sense God smile. His joy is my strength.

The Secret of Cooperative Learning Groups: A Facilitator

The leader's role in establishing Cooperative Learning Groups involves learning how to become a facilitator rather than a teacher. A facilitator is one who organizes activities in such a way that good things happen in groups of people – even if the facilitator is not the focal point of the activity. They create the occasion for God's people to bless, encourage, and coach each other in small groups. Turning the team loose with their workbooks and directions creates an atmosphere where the teacher may feel like they are teaching much less. However, the students are learning and growing much more. A teacher teaches but a facilitator leads. When a preacher preaches or a teacher teaches, the Holy

> **A teacher teaches but a facilitator leads.**

Spirit can move only through them. When a leader facilitates, the Holy Spirit can move through everyone! Don't misunderstand. We need preachers. I am one! We also need teachers. Imagine, though, how many more good things will happen among God's people when we properly prepare them with discipleship dynamics and then become facilitators by implementing these discipleship structures.

If you would like a more in-depth study on cooperative learning, order the book "Circles of Learning – Cooperation in the Classroom." Authors: David W. Johnson and Roger T. Johnson. ASCD Stock Number: 611:84324. ISBN: 0-87120-123-2. Library of Congress Card Catalog Number 83-093395. Though their concept of cooperative learning is designed for the public school classroom and is structured differently than what is presented here, the book was very instrumental in developing the discipleship dynamic of cooperative learning.

Structure #3
LARGE GROUP REVIEW

So far we have covered two discipleship structures:

1. Opening Discussion Groups are small groups of four to six people and are organized for discussion designed to help people get to know each other and introduce the session topic.
2. Cooperative Learning Groups are groups of two people that engage in various activities to help each other learn and grow.

The third discipleship structure is called Large Group Review. This structure takes place after the various small group activities and just before small group prayer. The whole group joins together in traditional rows or in a large circle. The leader now moderates the discussion and asks the group,

"What were your best insights from your study together?"

> **"What were your best insights from your study together?"**

Because of the small group interaction, people are ready to share. During this time the leader also shares their favorite insights and makes sure that students understood the main emphasis of the session.

The large group review is like a spiritual potluck and all the food is hot out of the oven. Everyone receives new insights from one another. Less mature groups gain insights from the more mature groups. People feel validated by being able to share and be heard. The leader feels the heartbeat of the group. The group also hears the heart of the leader. The Holy Spirit will often move over the group collectively at this time by resonating strong spiritual themes.

The leader plays an important role in making this time vibrant. Before sharing your thoughts, allow others to share theirs. Ask people to share only their most important point rather than giving several. This will allow others opportunity to share. Lead from your heart as well as your head. Be free to engage in emotions appropriate to the content being shared. Be enthusiastic about what the team has learned. Finally, use this time to build momentum for the small group prayer time that will take place after the large group review.

Chapter 11 provides valuable helps on leading large group conversations.

Structure #4
CONFIRMATION OF PROGRESS

Confirmation of Progress includes taking the unit test and verifying that the unit objectives were achieved.

This structure acts like a gas gauge. It shows if each student is "full" of the information. After all, people can only share what they have. The better they know it and the better it is logged into their long-term memory, the better they are able to confidently share the information with others.

Here is another benefit of this structure. If people know that others will see their progress, they will make sure there progress is something worth looking at. If people working on an assembly line know that someone will inspect their work, they do it better than if no one cares. This structure prods people to move beyond idly wishing that their spiritual tank was full. This structure helps motivate people to fill their tank! If people know they are going to be tested, they will study. If the information is not important enough to confirm with a test that they know it, they will not study.

The unit test makes our learning not only important but also urgent. After all, everyone agrees that knowing God's Word is important. However, most never get around to studying it well enough to share because so many "urgent things" get in the way. However, if there is a test on May 15, suddenly study becomes urgent on May 13 and 14. That is a good thing. Most of life's urgencies have little to do with God's eternal Kingdom. This one does!

Why is this way of thinking so foreign to God's church? Let's face it – it is because most people (leaders included) have a distorted theology of God's mercy and grace. To them, mercy means that God will not punish them for anything for which they deserve punishment. Grace means that God will give blessings for things that are completely undeserved. Therefore, there is no sense in making any real effort for God. Effort doesn't matter. In fact, if you do exert effort, you may be trying to earn your salvation by works rather than receiving it by faith. Therefore, accountability to God or others for personal progress in spiritual things is a completely foreign concept. More than that, it may be even considered doctrinal error.

We need to get our doctrine right. We are forgiven for our sins and adopted into God's family as His dear children by grace through faith. However, God's Word also says,

> Do your best to present yourself to God as one approved, a workman who does not need to be ashamed and who correctly handles the word of truth." *2 Timothy 2:15*

Children are children regardless of their works. However, if they are also going to serve in their father's company, they must do their best or they are going to be ashamed. The father and others will expect them to carry their weight and do their job well. Their role as children is one thing. Their role as workers is another. Too many of God's children don't understand this point. And yet, they wonder why they don't feel right on the inside. They wonder why they still feel so unworthy. People tell them that it is just the devil lying to them. This may be true at times. However, many Christians feel unworthy and ashamed because they not doing their best for God. They are not doing what God expects them to do. If we help them understand this and provide ways for them to correct the matter, they will experience more of God's joy and more confidence. They will also learn how to correctly handle the word of truth.

> **We need to get our doctrine right.**

Some people will balk at first at the thought of a test. If we explain it rightly, they will gain a completely new point of view and charge into the test rather than run from it. Let's do that! This structure makes people's progress important enough to measure. Quite frankly, our progress is very important to God. Let's make it important to us also. Look how important diligence and progress was to the Apostle Paul when writing to Timothy.

> Be diligent in these matters; give yourself wholly to them, so that everyone may see your progress. *1 Timothy 4:15*

Your role in establishing the discipleship structure is vital. Your heart and attitude toward this new challenge will affect many others. The workbook suggests proper times and ways to inform people about the test. It also provides direction to help those who may have some initial fear of a test. Show them that the test, an answer page and even a practice test are in the student's manual. There needn't be any stress about wondering what they will be expected to know.

As mentioned above, help your students develop a proper theology about works and preparation. Of course, like everything else, let them know that you will be taking the test with them. As their partners grade their test, you will have a partner grade yours. Finally, let people know that if their nerves make them freeze up and do poorly, they may retake the test. The goal is not to fail anyone. The goal is to help people truly learn and succeed.

Structure #5
MINISTRY REPORTING

Ministry Reporting is a time for students to communicate their progress in sharing the learned information with others. Time is provided for these reports near the end of many of the sessions.

Ministry reports may be given in the small groups of two, the groups of eight, or the whole class. The leader may adjust the format depending on the need, the time available, and leading of the Holy Spirit.

Though everyone is encouraged and expected to report on their ministry opportunities, sometimes it does not work out within the time frame given. In fishing terms, sometimes people get "skunked." For those unfamiliar with the term, it means they did not catch any fish. If this happens, it is up to the leader's discretion to either simply encourage them to share when they can or to provide future times for more reporting on this specific issue.

Ministry Reporting Time has many benefits. It helps people realize that sharing God's Word with others is just as important as learning His Word. It provides personal attention and encouragement for those endeavoring to share their faith. The personal attention to sharing raises the level of significance of sharing with others. It creates a positive mutual accountability to be doers of Christ's Word rather than just hearers. It provides opportunities to encourage each other. It generates godly excitement and enthusiasm for evangelism. It focuses the group's heart and prayers on reaching the lost. People go beyond learning just for the sake of learning and engage in learning for the sake of sharing it with others. This occasion will make the team more intentional in their preparation and prayer. Actual reporting on progress will create positive stress that produces action on the front end of the effort and positive celebration after the effort.

Here are steps you can take to make this time effective and positive:

1. Realize that everyone in your group already desires to share their faith. God has given them that desire. God will help them fulfill that desire. God is using you as a tool to equip and encourage them.

2. Help the team develop the discipleship dynamic of Intentional Sharing. Make sure that the large group wrap-up times and the small group prayer include this emphasis.

3. Take a genuine interest in people's progress in sharing their faith with others.

4. When people give their reports, remind them of the value of confidentiality. While it is good to celebrate progress in sharing with others, it is not good to divulge personal information without permission. Everyone should practice our Lord's golden rule to do to others only as we would want them to do to us. Remember that what may be considered a prayer request by one person may be considered gossip or a betrayal of a confidence by the person being discussed.

You and your team will enjoy this time together. It will be like putting logs on a fire. It will strengthen your joy for the advancement of the Gospel. It will increase your concern for the lost. It will also provide a clear sense of progress towards the goal of reaching them. This is what you are working for! May you sense God's Spirit imparting these dynamics to you and your team as you engage in ministry reports together.

Structure #6
UNIT COMPLETION

The Unit Completion is the session following the unit test and is dedicated to celebrating everyone's progress. Students who worked hard and did well receive recognition for their effort. Honor is given to whom honor is due. Team members share how they have grown and comment on the growth they observed in others. Certificates are presented to all who accomplished the main objectives of the course. Refreshments and fellowship can also be added as a way to celebrate the occasion.

The benefits of the unit completion are many. Celebrating progress refreshes hearts. It is encouraging and motivating. It is far more life-giving than motivation by guilt. This activity provides the group an opportunity to build each other up in love and to celebrate each other's accomplishment as well as their own. People gain a greater sense of significance for their time together. When something becomes significant, it creates personal diligence. Legitimate celebration greatly enhances team morale. High morale creates stronger faith and love than low morale. The joy of achievement becomes greater than the stress of the effort. It bonds the team together in its purpose and mission. The course leaders receive a glimpse of the fruit of their labors. Finally, celebration bestows the Lord's happiness on people for work well done.

> **Legitimate celebration greatly enhances team morale.**

As the leader of the group, you can do many things to make this celebration a rewarding experience. The workbook will provide the direction. Make adjustments to fit the needs of your group. The very first step of preparation is to prepare your heart. Get excited about the progress of your group. Ask God to use you to be an ambassador for Him in expressing His joy over their progress. Be generous with your heart and time to celebrate their progress. Organize the graduation in advance and let the group know what is happening. Enlist the help of others. Let someone who likes photography take the group picture. Ask them to make and distribute copies. Let others organize the refreshments. As you enlist the help of others, you give them the opportunity to be involved and needed. It also gives you the opportunity to be focused on people rather than on all the details.

Why make it such a big deal? Because the eternal things of God are a bigger deal than the temporal things of this world. Celebration communicates love and significance. It shows that people's progress matters to God and matters to you. This time will enrich your discipleship experience together.

Structure #7
PROMOTING THE NEXT STEP

Promoting the next step helps the team look ahead. It helps people see how far they have come and prepares their minds and hearts to continue their progress towards the final goal. In short, it keeps the ball rolling.

Promoting the next step supports the discipleship dynamic of clear vision for continued progress. It helps people see the big picture. It helps people stay on track with God. Promoting the next step creates forward thinking rather than just inward thinking, present tense or past tense thinking. It helps people prepare their minds for continued action. It capitalizes on the present momentum and uses it for further progress.

The *Fishers of Men* Series Preview (located on page 24) provides this "big picture" for all to see. It is a map to help the team see each unit as a step towards their goal of becoming well-equipped and effective witnesses for Christ.

As the leader of the group, begin promoting the next units early enough to get people signed up and books ordered so that there is no lull between each unit. The workbooks include announcements at appropriate times to help you. Help the group see what they have already accomplished and the goals that lie ahead. They will feel oriented instead of lost. They will have a sense of direction instead of wandering aimlessly. It provides purpose and a sense of personal achievement. These inner dynamics motivate people to keep on going for God. They build a mindset that prepares people for long-term commitment to the Lord.

Help your team imagine the humor of the disciples asking Jesus how long his discipleship would take? Think of how it would look if they requested a four-week mini-series – one night a week for forty five minutes or so. Then laugh.

> **Promoting the next step helps the team look ahead.**

Help your group remember the lesson learned in the fable of the three little pigs: Houses built with sticks and straw take far less time and work. They just don't last. We are building with brick! The next unit is the next row of bricks.

If the leadership role becomes too much for you to handle, ask someone else to help you or to lead the group. This would give you a break and allow others the opportunity to use their leadership. Having others ready to lead also helps you if you are on vacation or have to be out of town.

Finally, to take the leadership in promoting the next step, use your calendar. Plot out the projected sessions, the graduation and the new series date. Exercising foresight will inspire confidence in your leadership and help you help others take a great journey for God.

Reflections on
DISCIPLESHIP STRUCTURES

To create a different end product, we must revamp the factory. Discipleship structures are like stations in the factory. They are the way we organize people and our educational time together. Most preaching and teaching structures organize people in rows of chairs to listen to an instructor. Fishers of Men discipleship structures move people out of the passive large group and into smaller interactive groups. Here they are given well-defined activities and time allotments to accomplish small steps of achievement towards the larger goal.

1. **Opening Discussion Groups** build relationships and generate interest for the topic at hand.

2. **Cooperative Learning Groups** engage in a variety of activities where groups of two help each other learn and grow. Using the workbook and leader's direction, they coach one another for personal improvement. During these Personal Coaching Times:

    a. They review key information to log it into their long-term memory and settle it in their heart.

    b. They memorize Scripture and become skillful with God's Word.

    c. Small group discussion increases insight and builds relationships.

    d. Students pursue unit goals and objectives in a step-by-step process together so that they make incremental achievement.

    e. Groups approach the Lord together in small group prayer.

> **To create a different end product, we must revamp the factory.**

3. **Large Group Review** provides the opportunity for the whole group to benefit from the best insights of the class.

4. **Confirmation of Progress** shows everyone that their progress is important enough to measure and confirm.

5. **Ministry Reporting** provides attention to sharing the information learned rather than just learning the information.

6. **Unit Completion** motivates the team to excellence and celebrates the progress of all.

7. **Promoting the Next Step** capitalizes on the present momentum and provides direction for continuing the journey.

These are the *Fishers of Men* discipleship structures. They work together with the discipleship dynamics and create an interactive discipleship experience where people help each other learn and grow. As leaders learn this new style of interactive discipleship they teach less but the group learns more. As students become comfortable with this kind of interaction in the classroom, it prepares them to help others outside the classroom. All this leads to the desired end product - a team of people who know enough, dare enough, care enough to catch men's hearts for Christ.

Congratulations! You just learned about discipleship dynamics and discipleship structures. Now let's look at discipleship tools.

To obtain better results, we must engage in better activities.

Chapter 9

DISCIPLESHIP TOOLS

TO COMPLETE THE WORK

Discipleship tools are like the hammers, screwdrivers, and wrenches needed to assemble the end product. People serious about a project always prepare themselves by purchasing the right tools and learning how to use them. Some discipleship tools help people learn. Others help them remember. Some help students focus in the right direction, measure their progress, or confirm that they have truly learned what they set out to learn. Finally, the same tools that help them learn can also be used to help others learn. Let's open up the tool box and look inside.

Discipleship Tool #1
THE FISHERS OF MEN TRAINING MANUAL

The Leader's Manual contains all the information needed for the leader to lead the course. This manual also displays the student's manual pages in appropriate places so that the leader sees what the student sees while teaching them. It also allows the leader to participate as a student in a small group.

The Student's Manual contains small group discussion questions and other directions to assist the students in small groups.

Chapter 9   Discipleship Tools to Complete the Work

FISHERS OF MEN
Discipleship Ministry For Relational Evangelism
http://fishersofmeninc.org/

Learn how to join together and prepare your heart to hear and follow Christ's call to be fishers of men

Unit One
Committing
TO HIS CALL

Leader's Manual

Scott J. Visser

Discipleship Tool #2

THE UNIT GOAL AND OBJECTIVES PAGE

The unit goal describes the general aim for the workbook. It answers the question, "Why are we meeting together?"

The unit objectives are the steps of progress required to help each student achieve the unit goal. These objectives are laid out in the following three categories:

1. Learning objectives
2. Personal growth objectives
3. Specific action objectives

Here are the benefits this tool offers:

1. It provides clear direction.
2. It unites the team with common purposes.
3. It mobilizes the team to make measurable progress.
4. It helps the team attain the goal.

Chapter 9 Discipleship Tools to Complete the Work

Taken from Fishers of Men Unit 2: Proclaiming the Promised Messiah

UNIT GOAL

To learn how to proclaim Christ

as God's Messiah promised by His prophets

because when people realize who Jesus is

they will listen to what He said.

LEARNING OBJECTIVES

Learn how to:

- Explain five key truths about Messianic Prophecy.
- Share seven key prophecies and their fulfillments by Christ.
- Share four reasons why prophecy is significant to our faith.

PERSONAL GROWTH OBJECTIVES

This unit will help you to experience

- Strengthened faith in Christ based on prophetic evidence.
- Confidence to share Messianic Prophecy with others.
- Increased motivation to share Christ through the prophets.

SPECIFIC ACTION OBJECTIVES

During this unit you will

- Tab key Messianic prophecies and fulfillments in your Bible.
- Use Personal Focus Cards to help you remember and learn.
- Share Messianic prophecy with at least one person.

Discipleship Tool #3
SMALL GROUP CORE VALUES

Small group core values are a list of principles and standards the group should be expected to understand and abide by. Using this tool will benefit your group in many ways:

1. It provides a common standard for all.
2. It deals with common personality problems *before* they happen.
    a. Overly-opinionated people will realize their effect on others and practice self-control.
    b. Emotionally needy people will realize that they are expected to stay on track with discipleship rather than to seek out counseling for their problems during small group time.
    c. People who divulge details about others are taught the importance of confidentiality.
3. When bad behavioral habits are exposed, discussed and rejected by the group before they happen, it creates the awareness that everyone will recognize them and it creates positive pressure for people to avoid them.
4. Building group consensus for good behavior based on wisdom rather than just rules creates more power to establish the behavior even when the leader is not present.
5. Good behavior alleviates potential agitation between people.
6. It increases the level of trust and respect between members.
7. It helps to create a safe atmosphere for people to "get real" with each other.
8. The atmosphere of trust and respect greatly improves the way people interact with one another. It is the secret behind whether people "open up" or "clam up."
9. These values will also help your team to better relate to others outside the group – even those they reach for Christ.

If new people attend the group, make sure they read and agree to your group's core values so that they also experience their benefits.

Help people "open up." Put this tool to work for you!

SMALL GROUP CORE VALUES

BECAUSE HOW WE TREAT ONE ANOTHER MATTERS

Group Attendance — *I will make this group a priority and call if I will be absent or late. I realize that my commitment has the power to encourage or discourage the commitment of others.*

Healthy Environment — *I will create a safe atmosphere where people can be honest, try new things, practice together, make mistakes, mispronounce words, and still be accepted, respected, and encouraged. These groups are not for "perfect" people; they are for people who want to learn and grow even if it means showing their imperfections.*

Confidentiality — *I will keep personal information regarding people's lives confidential within the group unless permission is given. Exceptions to this would be comments that indicate impending harm to one's self or others.*

Allowing for Differences — *I will allow differences of viewpoints or opinions as they may come up in conversations. God's Word is the last word on every issue. However, even then, our understanding of His Word often varies. Highly opinionated people who expect everyone to think exactly like them intimidate some, annoy others and shut down conversations. I agree not to do this.*

Cooperative Learning — *I will allow others to help me grow and learn while also doing my part to help others grow and learn.*

Staying on Track — *My partners came to this course to prepare to proclaim the promised Messiah. I will not distract them by raising unrelated topics for discussion.*

Cooperation — *I will cooperate with the facilitator rather than continuing small group conversations while he or she is trying to give new direction. If needed, I will continue our small group discussion after class rather than expecting the whole group to wait for us.*

Discipleship Tool #4

PERSONAL FOCUS CARDS (MEMORY CARDS)

Personal Focus Cards are pocket-sized cards that contain the memory verses and other key information provided in the unit. They are included in each workbook.

The Benefits of Using This Tool

1. They provide instant access to key information for continual study.
2. They keep God's Word on each student's heart during the day.
3. They help to turn "down time" into study time.
4. They help each student become skillful with God's Word.
5. They make a good discussion tool for talking with others.
6. They help us to obey God's direction given in Deuteronomy 6:6-8

These commandments that I give you today are to be upon your hearts. 7 Impress them on your children. Talk about them when you sit at home and when you walk along the road, when you lie down and when you get up. 8Tie them as symbols on your hands and bind them on your foreheads. 9Write them on the doorframes of your houses and on your gates.
Deuteronomy 6:6-8

Chapter 9   Discipleship Tools to Complete the Work

Taken from *Fishers of Men* Unit 2: Proclaiming the Promised Messiah

PERSONAL FOCUS CARDS

Memory verses supporting each point are located on the back side of each card.

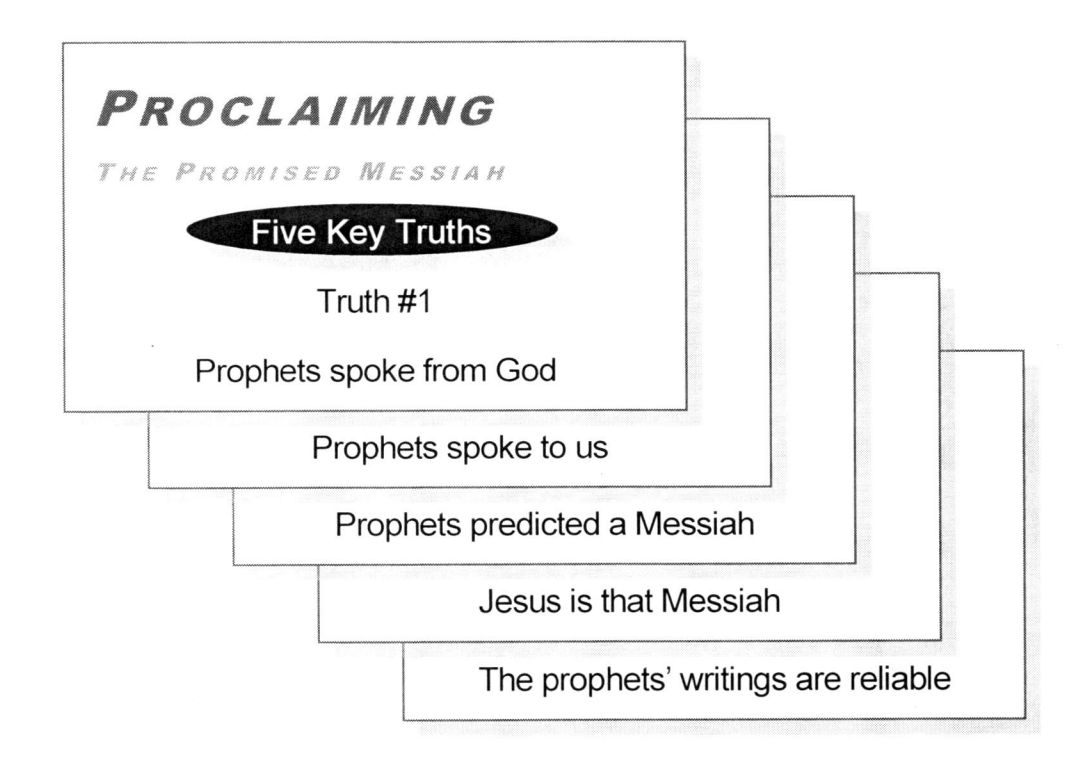

PROCLAIMING
THE PROMISED MESSIAH

Five Key Truths

Truth #1

Prophets spoke from God

Prophets spoke to us

Prophets predicted a Messiah

Jesus is that Messiah

The prophets' writings are reliable

Discipleship Tool #5
JOURNAL PAGES

A journal page is provided at the end of each session as an optional exercise for the students. Journaling can take on many different forms. It can be a note to one's self where students log their personal responses to the session. It could be used as a letter they write to themselves and read in the near future to help keep themselves motivated. Finally, this area may be used as space to write a prayer to the Lord in response to the lesson learned.

The Benefits of Using This Tool

1. Journaling clarifies our thoughts.
2. Journaling makes God's Word more personal.
3. Journaling deepens the impact of God's Word.
4. Journaling on God's Word creates an overflow of His Word in our hearts.
5. Thoughts that are journaled are easily shared with others.

Chapter 9 Discipleship Tools to Complete the Work

Taken from *Fishers of Men* Unit 2: Proclaiming the Promised Messiah

MY JOURNAL NOTES

DATE _____ TIME _____ PLACE _____

Discipleship Tool #6
THE UNIT TEST

The unit test measures each person's progress. It shows how well they learned the information. The test questions relate very closely to the unit goals and objectives.

The Unit Test provides these benefits:
1. A test motivates people to study.
2. It creates accountability to learn.
3. It shows students what they have learned.
4. It creates an occasion to celebrate.
5. It prepares people to share their faith with clarity and confidence.

Chapter 9 Discipleship Tools to Complete the Work

Taken from *Fishers of Men* Unit 2: Proclaiming the Promised Messiah

UNIT TEST
*ANSWER PAGE

1. State the Unit Goal. (5 points)
   *Answer: To prepare to proclaim Christ as God's Messiah promised by His prophets –
   because people need to realize who Jesus is before they will listen to what He said.*

2. Explain Messianic Prophecy. (5 points)
   Answer: Messianic Prophecy is specific predictions made by God's prophets about His coming Messiah.

3. What does the word, "Messiah" mean? (3 Points)
   *Answer: "Messiah" refers to a ruler and deliverer whom God will send to His people. Other titles that relate to
   the Messiah are the Anointed One, the Son of David and the Son of God.*

4. What is the New Testament Greek word that is equivalent to the Old Testament word for "Messiah"? (2 Points)   Answer: "Christ"

5. Explain the Five Key Truths About Messianic Prophecy with the references. (20 points total)
   (Give 2 points for each answer and 2 points for each reference.

   Answer:

Key Truth	Reference
1. Prophets spoke from God.	(2 Peter 1:20-21)
2. God's prophets spoke to us.	(1 Peter 1:12)
3. God's prophets predicted His Messiah	(1 Peter 1:10-11)
4. Jesus is that Messiah!	(Luke 24:44-47)
5. God's prophecies are reliable	(The Dead Sea Scrolls prove this)

Share seven Messianic Prophecies and their fulfillment by Christ (35 points are possible)

   (Give 5 points for each answer. You may use your tabbed Bible.)

Unit Test (Continued)

Answer:	Prediction	Fulfillment
1. A descendant of David	2 Samuel 7:12	Matthew 1:1
2. Born in Bethlehem	Micah 5:2	Matthew 2:1
3. Born of a virgin	Isaiah 7:14	Matthew 1:21-23
4. Have healing power	Isaiah 35:4-6	Acts 10:37
5. Rejected by His people	Psalm 118:22	Acts 4:9-11
6. Die for our sins	Isaiah 53:5	1 Corinthians 15:3
7. Be raised from the dead!	Psalm 16:8-10	Mark 16:6

7. Give four reasons why prophecy is significant. (20 points available)

    (Give 5 points for each correct answer.)

    Answer:

    1. Fulfilled prophecy confirms the apostles' testimony of Christ.

    2. Fulfilled prophecy provides statistical evidence that Jesus is the Messiah.

    3. Fulfilled prophecy places Scripture above other books.

    4. Fulfilled prophecy provides strong logical grounds for believing in Christ.

8. How did this study strengthen your faith in Christ? (5 points)

   _____

9. Has your confidence increased to share Messianic Prophecy with others? What helped you the most? (5 points)

   _____

Chapter 9   Discipleship Tools to Complete the Work

Discipleship Tool #7
PROGRESS POINTS PAGE

The Progress Points Page is laid out like a running course with specific steps that lead to the unit goal. Space is provided for a student's accountability partner to sign and date each completed step.

Listed below are several benefits this tool provides:

1. It provides a way to demonstrate voluntary accountability.
2. It measures incremental achievement.
3. It strengthens the student's awareness of personal progress.
4. It provides a clear map for the journey.
5. It provides a destination point to achieve and celebrate.

The Progress Point Pages are shown on the next two page in full size for easier viewing.

PROGRESS POINTS

TO FULFILL THE VISION

Therefore, since we are surrounded by such a great cloud of witnesses, let us throw off everything that hinders and the sin that so easily entangles, and let us run with perseverance the race marked out for us. *Hebrews 12:1*

Working with an accountability partner from the group, check the boxes that show your progress.

- ☐ I browsed over this course and see that I need it.
- ☐ I believe Jesus wants me to learn these things.
- ☐ I will make this study a high priority for Christ.
- ☐ I will set aside time for this study at home.
- ☐ I learned five key truths about Messianic Prophecy.
- ☐ I tabbed five key truths in my Bible.
- ☐ I used the five key truths Personal Focus Cards.
- ☐ I learned the seven predictions and their fulfillments.
- ☐ I tabbed the seven predictions and fulfillments in my Bible.

Chapter 9 Discipleship Tools to Complete the Work

Do you not know that in a race all the runners run, but only one gets the prize? Run in such a way as to get the prize. ²⁵Everyone who competes in the games goes into strict training. They do it to get a crown that will not last; but we do it to get a crown that will last forever. ²⁶Therefore I do not run like a man running aimlessly; I do not fight like a man beating the air. *I Corinthians 9:24-26*

THE VISION

- I used the Seven Predictions Personal Focus Cards.
- I learned four reasons why prophecy is significant.
- I learned five ways to prepare for outreach in prayer.
- I passed the unit test with 70% or higher.
- I am prepared to proclaim Jesus as God's Messiah promised by His prophets.
- I shared Messianic Prophecy with someone else.
- I completed this unit!
- I promise the LORD to tell others what I learned.
- (Future date.) I led someone to faith in Christ.

THIS TRAINING WILL PREPARE YOU TO WIN YOUR RACE!

Discipleship Tool #8
MINISTRY REPORT PAGE

The Ministry Report Page is a form provided for students to write down their ministry opportunity.

This form helps students in the following ways:

1. It is a signal that sharing with others will be taken seriously rather than just mentioned with no follow-up.

2. It provides direction and space for students to report on their progress of telling others about what they learned.

3. It helps students walk out the discipleship dynamic of Intentional Sharing.

4. It supports the dynamic of Voluntary Accountability.

5. It provides for an occasion of Celebration of Progress.

Chapter 9 Discipleship Tools to Complete the Work

Taken from *Fishers of Men* Unit 3: Telling God's Good News

MINISTRY REPORT PAGE

FOR UNIT 2: PROCLAIMING THE PROMISED MESSIAH

Reporting Guidelines

Remember to be confidential. Do not share personal information that could later be taken as betraying a confidence or as gossip.

Here is what I said to my friend.

_____

_____

_____

This was their response.

_____

_____

Questions I have about their response.

_____

_____

What I will share with them next time I get the chance.

_____

_____

Discipleship Tool #9

CERTIFICATES OF COMPLETION

Certificates of Completion are a token of recognition for each person's progress. Three levels of certification are provided in most books. Each represents a different level of achievement. These include a Certificate of Participation, a Certificate of Completion with Honors, and a Certificate of Completion with Excellence.

The Benefits of Using This Tool

1. It gives students a tangible goal to pursue.
2. It provides a lasting token of each student's accomplishment.
3. It shows the leader's attention and care for each student's progress.
4. It celebrates students' achievements.
5. If displayed, the certificate serves as a reminder to share the truth learned.

Note: The Certificate of Completion with Excellence is displayed on the right page. The Certificate of Completion with Honors and the Certificate of Participation are not shown.

FISHERS OF MEN
Discipleship Ministry For Relational Evangelism
CERTIFICATE OF COMPLETION

Presented to

_____

In recognition of your
COMPLETION WITH EXCELLENCE
in *Fishers of Men* - Unit 2

PROCLAIMING
THE PROMISED MESSIAH

at

on the date of

_____

Facilitator _____

"Come, follow me," Jesus said, "And I will make you fishers of men."
At once they left their nets and followed Him.   Matthew 4:19-20

Fishers of Men Inc. 7755 N. Carefree Drive, Whitehall, MI 49461 (231) 215-5406   http://fishersofmeninc.org

Discipleship Tool # 10
INVITATION TO TAKE THE NEXT STEP

The invitation to take the next step encourages students to continue in their discipleship process towards relational evangelism. It promotes the next unit and provides a glimpse of what the unit offers. Though this invitation is placed in the back of the workbook, the lesson plan includes an invitation several weeks earlier in the series in order to provide time for people to sign up, and arrangement made for books to be ordered.

INVITATION
TO FISHERS OF MEN – UNIT 3 TITLED

Telling God's Good News

NOW THAT YOU ARE ABLE TO SHOW PEOPLE
WHO JESUS IS,
GET READY TO TELL OTHERS
WHAT HE SAID.

FISHERS OF MEN
Discipleship Ministry For Relational Evangelism

Learn how to help people be reconciled to God by putting their faith in Jesus His Son.

Unit Three
Telling God's Good News
Leader's Manual

Scott J. Visser

Order your books at http://fishersofmeninc.org

Chapter 10

FITTING IT ALL TOGETHER

Here is a brief overview of the thoughts covered so far:

1. We need to engage in relational evangelism. Jesus said sheep run from strangers.

2. We need to prepare for relational evangelism with a clear end in mind.

3. That end is to develop people who know enough, dare enough, care enough to catch men's hearts for Christ.

4. The *Fishers of Men* units displayed on page 24 are designed to equip people to obtain that end.

5. Here is a reality check: People need experiential interactive discipleship if they are going to become skilled in God's Word.

6. They need a coach - someone who will help them make progress.

7. To build a new product, we need a new factory.

8. This new discipleship factory has new dynamics, structures, and tools.

9. The chart on the next page shows how they fit together to help students achieve the unit outcome and the series outcome.

10. The second chart on the following page provides a simple comparisonG between the *Fishers of Men* discipleship format and the usual teaching format.

Chapter 10 Fitting All Together

UNIT OUTCOME

Students are able to share the Unit's life-changing information with others from their head and their heart.

→

SERIES OUTCOME

To raise up a team of people who know enough, dare enough, and care enough to catch men's hearts for Christ.

Discipleship Tools

TO COMPLETE THE WORK

1. The Fishers of Men Manual
2. Unit Goal and Objectives
3. Small Group Core Values
4. Personal Focus Cards
5. Journal Pages
6. Unit Test
7. Progress Points Page
8. Ministry Report Page
9. Certificate of Completion
10. Invitation to Take the Next Step

Discipleship Structures

PROMOTE PROGRESS

1. Opening Discussion Groups
2. Cooperative Learning Groups
   a. Small Group Discussion
   b. Personal Coaching Time
      - Scripture Memory Work
      - Review Key Information
      - Communication Practice
      - Pursue Unit Goal/objectives
        - Study for the Unit Test
   c. Small Group Prayer
3. Large Group Review
4. Progress Confirmation
5. Ministry Reporting Time
6. Unit Completion
7. Promoting the Next Step

Discipleship Dynamics

ENLIGHTEN AND ENERGIZE THE EFFORT

1. Getting Real
2. Incremental Achievement
3. Small Group Interaction
4. Voluntary Accountability
5. Intentional Sharing
6. Celebration of Progress
7. Clear Vision for Continued Progress
8. Courage to Take New Steps

119

The *Fishers of Men* Discipleship Format

is like coaching a football team and practicing before playing the game.

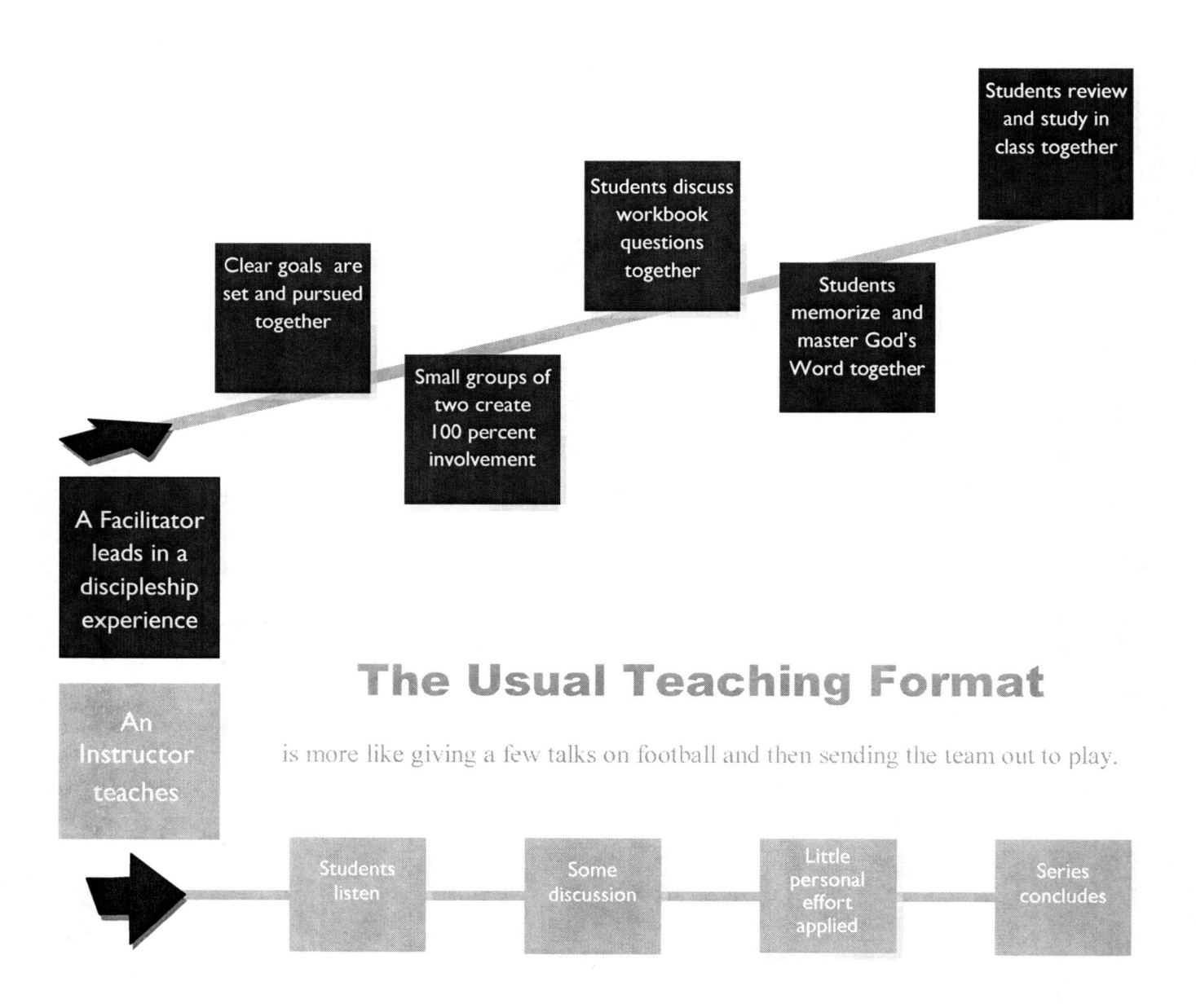

- A Facilitator leads in a discipleship experience
- Clear goals are set and pursued together
- Small groups of two create 100 percent involvement
- Students discuss workbook questions together
- Students memorize and master God's Word together
- Students review and study in class together

The Usual Teaching Format

is more like giving a few talks on football and then sending the team out to play.

- An Instructor teaches
- Students listen
- Some discussion
- Little personal effort applied
- Series concludes

Chapter 10   Fitting All Together

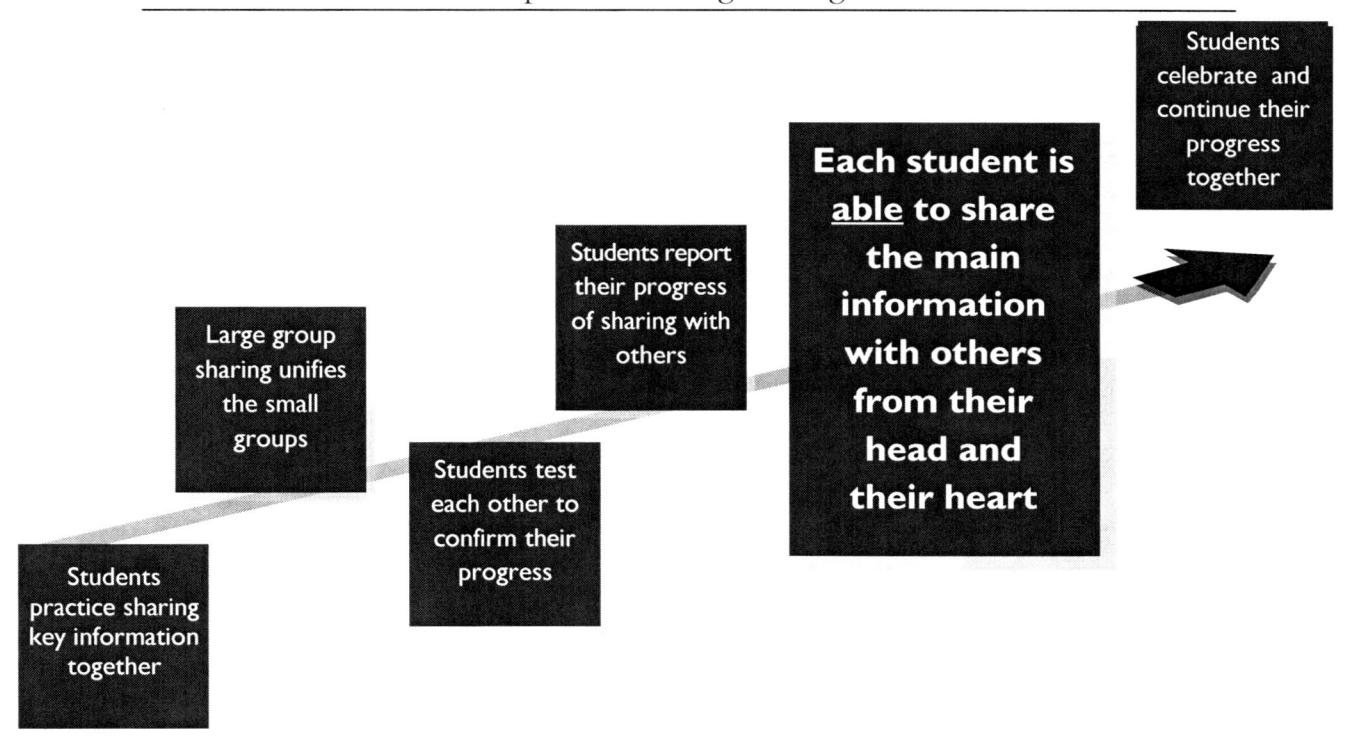

- Students practice sharing key information together
- Large group sharing unifies the small groups
- Students test each other to confirm their progress
- Students report their progress of sharing with others
- **Each student is <u>able</u> to share the main information with others from their head and their heart**
- Students celebrate and continue their progress together

If you were competing with the devil

for the souls of men

and "the score" lasted for eternity,

which training format would you choose?

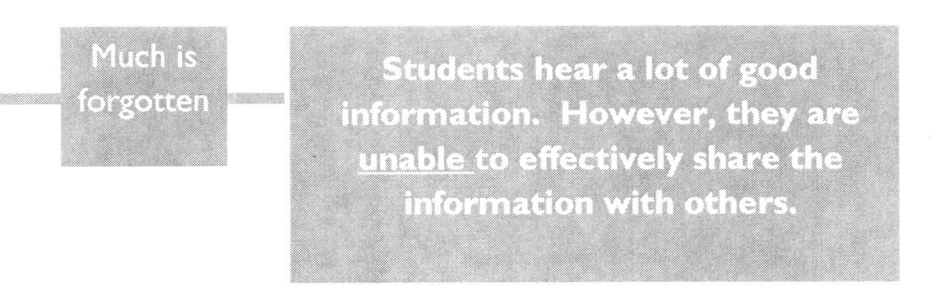

Much is forgotten — Students hear a lot of good information. However, they are <u>unable</u> to effectively share the information with others.

121

Chapter 11

LEADERSHIP SKILLS

Just as a new factory requires new steps of maintenance, new discipleship structures create new issues that leaders must manage. Knowing about them ahead of time and being prepared will enable you to better serve those you lead. Here are five leadership skills to equip you for work ahead.

Leadership Skill #1
MANAGING SMALL GROUP ISSUES

Small groups are a wonderful structure and provide many benefits. Learning how to deal with some common small group issues will make them even better.

Issue #1. Helping poor readers and slow learners

Small groups provide no place to hide if people are poor readers. Even good readers cannot pronounce certain names and some words in the Bible. Address this issue ahead of time. Let them know that you cannot pronounce them either. This is one of those places where everyone needs to determine that they are not going to let that stop them. Saying the words incorrectly is better than not reading Scripture together.

If people are poor readers, this course will give them plenty of exercise to improve. Furthermore, what better reason to learn how to read than to learn how to share the Good News with others. If they can't read well enough to read aloud, encourage them to dare to say, "Hey, I never learned to read well. Would you read while I follow along?"

I have led groups where one man helped the other learn how to read better while taking the class together. Their pace was slower. They met together on another night for extra study. Within a few months, the man who read at a second grade level could read the material easily. He not only learned how to become a fisher of men; He overcame a life-long obstacle. Creating a safe atmosphere for people to take off their masks, face their weaknesses and start at that point together brings real progress. If we help people get over their fear and their embarrassment and help each other, good things happen.

Working with a poor reader or slower learner requires a little more patience. Consider allowing a group to work together as a threesome if one member is a slow learner. It takes the pressure off, allows them to say less and listen a little more while the other two in the group do more of the interacting.

Issue #2. Encouraging Different Group Partners

It is human nature for most people to stay with the same partners. However, encourage people to change partners for different activities. It helps them to get to know everyone in the large group. It keeps one person from possibly latching on to another person and not allowing them to connect with others. It exposes everyone to a wide variety of personalities. It stretches the group out of their usual social comfort zones. If God's people are going to reach out to others in this world, they must become comfortable with the stretching process. Finally, if there are some slower learners, a few of the more capable and mature people in the group can share the responsibility.

Issue #3. Navigating the Male and Female Mix

If your group contains males and females you may want to discuss their preference in this area. It all depends on the nature of your group. In most groups this will not be a problem. In some groups you may have to give direction.

Chapter 11   Leadership Skills

Issue #4. Helping People Initiate Conversations

If the group is new to small groups, it will be awkward for some to initiate your direction once in their group. They will be asking the question inside, "Should I start the conversation or should I allow my partner to start?" You can solve this challenge quickly and easily by giving some general direction. Here are some suggestions:

1. Let the oldest person begin the discussion this time or,

2. Let the youngest person begin or,

3. Let the person whose birthday is nearest to today begin the conversation.

Once people are comfortable with small groups, this direction will not be necessary.

Issue #5. Encouraging Mutual Leadership

Some people are natural leaders. Others simply always want to be in charge. Others never want to lead. However, part of the discipleship process is to help people become comfortable in taking initiative in conversations and providing small steps of leadership. As people gain these skills, they will be better equipped to lead others to Christ. Therefore, direct the groups to alternate in the leadership roles throughout the small group times. One person should lead the conversation in one workbook question. The other person should lead in the next.

Leadership Skill #2
MANAGING THE CLOCK

One of the most important responsibilities as a coach is to manage time well. If you do, the group will accomplish the unit goals and objectives in a reasonable amount of time. Here are some suggestions to help develop this skill:

1. Know the goals and objectives, communicate them to the team and provide the class time to work on them together.

2. Use the session introduction to clearly communicate what the group will be doing in the session. If they know where you are leading they will be less likely to lead you and the group down rabbit trails with unrelated questions.

3. If someone raises an issue that has nothing to do with the session's direction, say to them, "That is a great question but it is not the direction for this session. I will be glad to talk with you after the session." The group will appreciate your leadership. It will also set a standard. Others will be less likely to repeat the behavior.

4. If individuals habitually raise questions outside the scope of the course, raise the issue with the group. Ask everyone to keep their questions and comments in focus with the discussion at hand. If everyone directs their thoughts in the same direction, the team will make far more progress than if everyone is thinking in different directions.

5. Another way you can manage the clock is to ask people to stay conscious of the time. Agree to avoid long stories that take forever to get to the point. That may keep the group from completing their work.

6. Help the groups understand that sometimes the slowest group will have to cut their conversation short so that they do not hold up the whole class. Explain this ahead of time so that there are no hurt feelings.

7. If possible provide a large clock that everyone can see. A small pleasant-sounding alarm that gives a one-minute warning for people to wrap-up will also help you engage in a small group conversation without continually needing to watch the clock.

8. If the majority of groups need more time, provide it – even if it means not completing the session. Quality learning is better than rushing.

9. If the Spirit of God is moving deeply on people's hearts in a conversation, do not feel pressured to rush Him! Allow more time for that conversation or activity.

The age-old question is, "What do you do if you run out of time?" Some teachers will quickly pack in thirty minutes of information into a five-minute period. The problem is, that information really did not "get in" anywhere. It may have vibrated eardrums but it did not seep into minds and hearts. That kind of rushing is like sweeping a large dirty floor in forty-five seconds. Someone went through the motions but the floor is not clean.

Here is a question we all need to ask ourselves, "What is more important: spending a certain amount of time on a unit goal and objectives or completing them?" Any other builder or manufacturer would never work on a project for a predetermined amount of time and walk away from it unfinished. They would work it out so that their project was completed. Some projects take less time than planned. Others take more. Wherever they left off on the project at the end of one day, they would naturally pick up from that point on the next. Skipping parts of the project is not an option. The same should be true with discipleship for our Lord Jesus Christ. Therefore, if you run out of time simply draw a line in your notes and start there next time.

What is more important: spending a certain amount of time on a unit goal and objectives or completing them?

Leadership Skill #3
LEADING LARGE GROUP DISCUSSIONS

The *Fishers of Men* Leader's Manual provides basic questions for all of the discussion times. However, the more skilled you become at leading discussion, the higher quality discussions you will have. Here are some general guidelines for asking discussion questions:

1. **Avoid questions requiring a "yes" or "no" answer.**
   They do not make for good conversation.

2. **Ask open-ended questions.**
   Open-ended questions promote discussion because they are non-threatening. There is no wrong answer to this style of question. They open windows into how people think and create potential for gaining new insights. It also opens the door for you to share how you think. Here are some examples of open-ended questions:
   - "What does this verse make you think of?"
   - "How do you suppose they felt in this story?"
   - "What do you think God is saying to your heart through these Scriptures?"

3. **Ask Review Questions.**
   Review questions confirm that key information was learned. The Unit Test is comprised mainly of review questions. These questions are looking for a specific answer. Here are some examples of review questions:
   - What three main points did we learn about prophecy?
   - What New Testament word is equivalent to the Old Testament word for Messiah?

4. Involve many rather than a few.

Every class typically has one or two over-zealous students who would answer every question if you let them. This stifles group involvement. Let them know that you appreciate their willingness to answer questions but that you really want to hear from the whole group. On occasion, let the more quiet people know that you value their thoughts also. Direct specific questions towards them.

Leadership Skill #4
HANDLING COMMON DISCUSSION SITUATIONS

Large group discussions provide many benefits. However, inviting a group to discuss an issue is more risky than talking about it yourself. Here are common issues that may arise along with suggestions for handling them:

Situation #1: The group seems slow to answer the question.

Group silence brings such dread to some leaders that they answer their question themselves rather than wait any longer for a response. From that point on, they avoid asking the group any more questions and revert to the safer lecture style of delivery. Here are ways to deal with this issue:

a. Remember, the group has not thought about the topic beforehand like you have. They may need a minute to collect their thoughts.
b. Make sure you have developed a safe atmosphere for group discussion by discussing small group core values.
c. Make sure that the group clearly understands the question.
d. Restate the question in a little different way.
e. People may need to be asked specifically for their response rather than waiting for them to volunteer it – especially at first.

The good news is that in the *Fishers of Men* format, large group discussions follow small group discussions on the same topic. Therefore, the group is ready to share their thoughts.

Situation #2: Someone gives a "wrong" answer.

Let's face it - groups of people contain a wide range of maturity. Be comfortable with that. Also be very careful about embarrassing people publicly. If you do, you will not only shut them down, you will make many others less likely to offer their thoughts for fear of the same consequences. Here are some possible ways to respond to a wrong answer.

- "Thanks for sharing. Like everything else, there are probably some other viewpoints on this too. Let's hear them also."
- "I have felt like that before also, but then…" (Tell how you came to see it differently.)
- Sometimes people give the wrong answer because they misunderstood the question. If so, thank them for their input and restate the question.

Situation #3: The discussion turns into a debate.

Differing views can be very healthy. However, if the topic begins to polarize the group, get heated or take up more time than what you feel the Lord desires, then it is time to provide leadership. Here are a few possible responses:

- "Let's make sure we practice discussing things rather than debating them. Discussion allows us to learn new information and gain new perspectives. They involve talking and listening and being open to change. Debates signal that our mind is already made up and we are not open to hear others out."
- "I can see that we are not going to resolve this in this session. Nor do I feel it is the direction the Lord is leading us, so we are going to have to let this discussion go for now and get back on to the main topic." (From there, give leadership by asking a key question or making key points to lead the conversation.)
- "I am not a theologian on such matters. I am going to defer that issue to our pastor to discuss or answer your questions."

Situation #4: You want the group to discuss a point further.

Sometimes people make a great comment and you feel there is more to be said about it. Here are some ways to do so:

a. Thank them for their insight.
b. Ask if others had similar insights on that topic.
c. Briefly share your insights on the same topic

Situation #5: The group drifts off the topic.

We all know how easily that can happen. Here are some ways to respond:

- "It seems we have drifted off the topic. Let's get back on track with our direction for this session. What do you think about …"
- "That would be really interesting to talk about but right now I think the Lord wants us to stay on track with the topic of …"

Situation #6: You do not know the answer for a question.

That situation can be very uncomfortable for some. In fact, this is a common reason people don't engage in conversations about their faith in Christ. However, remember this: you do not have to know everything in order to help others. You need only to share what you *do know*. Here are some tips for handling questions for which you do not know the answer:

a. Don't pretend to know the answer.
b. Don't be embarrassed for not knowing the answer. No one knows everything.
c. Let them know that they have a very good question.
d. Ask others in the group for their thoughts on the topic
e. If need be, let them know that you will get back with them after a little more research. Get help from others.

As you gain skill and grow comfortable in leading large group conversations, you will become more like a shepherd who knows how to lead sheep to green pastures to eat and quiet waters to drink. You will be used by God to facilitate conversation times where people truly build one another up in love.

Leadership Skill #5
CHOOSING EFFECTIVE SEATING ARRANGEMENTS

Just as the session time has been structured in new ways to accomplish a new outcome, seating arrangements are modified to accommodate the activity. Seating arrangements make a big difference on how the group interacts with the leader and each other. Here are four different arrangements used in the *Fishers of Men* sessions:

1. Rows of chairs

This arrangement is the most efficient for fitting a large group of people into a relatively small space. It serves the preaching and large group lecture setting well because it focuses everyone's attention on the speaker.

2. One large circle

A circle of twenty-five or less allows people to see everyone's face rather than the backs of heads. Therefore, it is a better choice if you desire interaction between the students during the large group discussion times.

3. Circles of four to eight

Circles of four to eight people accommodate opening discussion groups. This arrangement facilitates small group cooperation, intimacy, and bonding. When people share God's truth in smaller groups, it becomes more personal. When truth becomes more personal, it changes not only one's head but one's heart. Any size group can join in these circles as long as there is enough space in the room.

4. Groups of two

This arrangement is used at least 50% of the instructional time. Students face each other or sit side-by-side and engage in the small group exercises described in the workbook. Disburse these groups randomly throughout the room allowing space between groups for less distraction and more personal conversation.

Leadership Skill #6
OVERCOMING ATTENDANCE CHALLENGES

Commitment to discipleship is Christ's command – not just a good idea. We should be clear on that for His sake. This course is not designed for casual attendees any more than a sport team is built on people who occasionally show up for practice. Every team member must realize that their commitment affects not only themselves but the Lord who calls them and the rest of the team who depends on them. Our commitment affects the morale and commitment of others.

With all that understood, we must also realize that every person may not be able to make every session. Some have to travel for work. People will be on vacations or have to be out of town. If we provide some flexibility, people will be more likely to get involved.

Students can accomplish the unit goal and objectives without attending all the sessions. They can use their workbook outside of class as well as in class. They can meet with a small group partner on another evening, over the phone or online. All you have to do is make the way for them and keep them informed.

Encourage communication about attendance. Ask people to let you know if they are unable to make a session. It shows you care about them. It also shows that they care about you and the rest of the team. It shows that, even though they may not be able to be there, they still have the team and the cause in their hearts. That matters. People's care about the cause affects other people's morale and commitment. A quick phone call makes a big difference.

Leadership Skill #7
GRAFTING IN NEW PEOPLE

Within the first two or three weeks, people could join the course and catch up if they are willing to work at home. After that, it is better to close the class until the next unit begins. It would be awkward for students to include guests while studying information they have been working on together for weeks.

Still, people interested in the ministry should be enthusiastically invited to join the next unit. Though the units fit together in a logical progression, students do not need to take a previous unit in order to join the upcoming one.

As mentioned before, new students should be asked to preview and agree to the small group core values. New people will quickly learn the structures and the tools used. It would also be helpful, however, for someone to talk to them about the discipleship dynamics adopted by the group.

Chapter 12

OVERCOMING DISCIPLESHIP HANG-UPS

By now it is likely that many of your reservations about making disciples have already been settled. You realize Christ's call for discipleship, you understand the need, and you have a clear picture of how to go about it. That puts you miles ahead of most people. Still, there may be a few common inner reservations that may cause some to sit back and wait for others rather than step forward and take initiative. Here are common discipleship hang-ups and answers to help you overcome them.

Hang-up #1. A Negative Mindset About Discipleship

Some people picture discipleship as a cultish practice where the leader manipulates people and micromanages every aspect of their lives. They live in a commune and everyone ends up brainwashed and drinks poisoned Kool-aid® together. I know. It sounds negative to even bring it up but after cult leaders like David Kuresh in the seventies, some people view discipleship that way.

Answer

This discipleship effort is not like that. The discipleship program described here is coaching, mentoring, and joining together to help each other become better equipped to share God's Word with others. Jesus called us to make disciples regardless of what cults do with the concept. Let's be clear on that and help others be clear also. Discipleship is biblical.

Hang-up #2. Self-doubt

Self-doubt stops people dead in their tracks on the way to any journey. Self-doubt says, "Who am I to lead others?" It looks similar to humility but it is distorted on a few issues. First of all, who we are is not the issue. Who Jesus is is the issue. What He commanded is the issue. He is the Son of the living God. He commanded us to make disciples who would also love, trust and follow Him. That is the issue.

Answer

It is true. There may be better people than either of us to do the job. However, if all that is available to reach certain people in our sphere of influence is us – are we going to decline like everyone else? I'm not. I hope you're not either. We are not perfect by any stretch but, we are far better than nothing. Besides, don't you wish you would have had someone help you grow in the skills and confidence described in this ministry? Don't you wish someone else would have stepped up to the plate for you – even if they weren't perfect? I do. I can't change what others did not do for me. But I can change what I am willing to do for the Lord and others. Imperfection is far better than nothing. If we don't reach the people around us who will?

Hang-up #3. Feeling inadequate

Many people feel inadequate to make disciples.

Answer

The truth is, it is good to feel inadequate in ourselves. If we thought we had it all together, we would not have to trust God. We would be full of pride rather than having to trust the Lord for grace and help. Believe me – the Lord would rather have humble and needy people serving him rather than proud, self-sufficient ones any day.

Furthermore, this course is not about anyone pretending they have arrived. The very first discipleship dynamic of "getting real" lays the ground work for admitting that you have NOT arrived either. You have come to learn and grow like everyone else. There may be smarter people in the group. That's okay. You don't have to be the smartest person. You just have to be willing to organize a group and coach a team the best you can. Serving the Lord and helping others imperfectly is far better than doing nothing at all. What better way to encourage others to step out of their comfort zones to make progress with Jesus than by stepping out of yours with them?

Let your feelings of inadequacy drive you to take courage and trust the Lord.

Hang-up #4. Reluctant to make the commitment

I am so busy with so many other things.

Answer

Coaching a *Fishers of Men* group is a commitment to Christ and His church. Let me ask you, "What do you have better to do?" If He has called you to do something else, by all means, you should follow that call. However, please do not invest your time, effort and money on things that will not matter at all in the next decade let alone the next one hundred years. Their self-serving trivial pursuits do nothing to advance God's Kingdom. Reaching souls for Christ changes many lives – not just the one you reach but everyone around them. Think about this. If you lead a man to the Lord, his wife, children, family, co-workers and neighbors are affected. If you spend your time on lesser things, you will make a lesser effect. Here is how Jesus said it to the Apostle Paul:

> Now get up and stand on your feet. I have appeared to you to appoint you as a servant and as a witness of what you have seen of me and what I will show you. [17]I will rescue you from your own people and from the Gentiles. I am sending you to them [18]to open their eyes and turn them from darkness to light, and from the power of Satan to God, so that they may receive forgiveness of sins and a place among those who are sanctified by faith in me. *Acts 26:16-18*

Here's Paul's response.

"So then, ... I was not disobedient to the vision from heaven."

He didn't shrink from the call due to a lack of commitment. I pray that you and I don't either. There is no worldly goal, career, hobby, or interest that is higher than this one. Oh wait! Yes there is! If you prepare and equip others to do it with you, you multiplied your efforts! There is no effort that will bring more lasting fulfillment and joy. It is worth the commitment. Jesus is worthy of your commitment.

Hang-up #5. Doubt that others will commit

I wonder if other people will be committed.

Answer

Some will and some won't. The more you communicate the calling, the need, and the cause, the more likely it is that more people will commit. There are people in God's church who have yearned all their lives for an opportunity like this. They just did not know how to find it.

It is true that people don't want to "get all dressed up" if they have nowhere to go. However when people get a picture of what they can be for God and where they can go for Him, they get inspired to get dressed up for the journey. Look how people commit themselves to sports and causes that have no eternal consequence. They long to be committed to something that matters. People find significance and purpose in doing things that matter. Show them how much it matters and they will commit. Show them how it matters to Christ and they will take on the challenge for Him.

Chapter 12   Overcoming Discipleship Hangups

Hang-up #6. Concern about the cost

Fishers of Men materials cost more than courses that have no workbooks and no discipleship tools. In this world's economy, it might seem hard at first to ask people to invest in their discipleship. In fact, many people's first reaction may be to balk at buying a new workbook every other month.

Answer

Most people will go to a restaurant and a movie or invest in some hobby without a second thought. Challenge their thinking with this point. Anyone who goes fishing knows they have to buy the tackle and the lures. If this cause is not worthy of their investment, ask God to lead people to you who feel differently. Don't be timid because there is a cost. The Kingdom of God is worth the cost.

Hang-up #7. Concern about the time commitment

It seems like this course requires a lot time.

Answer

It takes approximately eight weeks to accomplish the goals and objectives given in each *Fishers of Men* unit. It is up to you to decide how many you do and if you take breaks between units. If you took all the courses one right after the other, you would easily have seventy weeks worth of material. With holidays, special services, and some breaks for fellowship and outreach, you will likely need eighteen months.

That seems like a long time. However, think about some events eighteen months ago. The time flew. This will too. Also, think about this: any quality effort that makes a lasting impact always requires quality time. This includes marriages, education, building a home, and other projects that last for years. Why would we think our part in God's Kingdom would require less? It is worth the time.

These are the common hang-ups that may hinder some from getting on board. I am no different from you or others. I have struggled through them all.

1. I've had a negative mindset about discipleship and have gotten over it.

2. Self-doubt at times hinder me until I get my eyes off from me.
3. I have felt inadequate but realize that His grace is not.
4. I wondered about the commitment – untill I saw the prize.
5. I thought maybe others would not commit. They did – and loved it!
6. I was concerned about the cost. God is not.
7. I worried about the time commitment. Right values produce right priorities.

Hang-up #8. It seems like people should just follow Jesus and He (not me) will make them fishers of men.

No. Jesus leads and empowers men and women to carry out that work today.

> It was he who gave some to be apostles, some to be prophets, some to be evangelists, and some to be pastors and teachers, to prepare God's people for works of service, so that the body of Christ may be built up. *Ephesians 4:11-12*

Each hindrance has the power to stop people dead in their tracks. There are likely other hang-ups that have not been mentioned. Still, if we desire to succeed, we can "get over it" so we are not "under it" so that we` can "get on with it." I am praying that you do. We have enough people in this world full of good intentions and empty of good action. Let's get going for God!

Don't you wish someone had helped you become a fisher of men for Christ – even if they were not perfect? You can be that person for someone else.

Chapter 13

STARTING

A *FISHERS* OF *MEN* GROUP

If you are still reading, congratulations! You must be serious. Starting a *Fishers of Men* group will be one the most rewarding journeys of your life. You will be taking steps to obey the Lord and make disciples. He will bless you. Here are some steps to help you with the process:

Step #1. Begin with Prayer

Any journey begun with prayer goes better than one that didn't. If you seek the Lord in prayer, He will give you the direction you need, He will give you the power you need, and He will provide the resources you need. Share your heart with those close to you that are given to prayer. Ask them to be praying for you and for the Lord's will to prosper in your hands for His sake. Let prayer prepare the spiritual atmosphere for a season. Gather people together for prayer at your home. It will make a big difference if you are not too hasty and truly begin with prayer.

Step #2. Provide Adequate Promotional Time

One of the most common mistakes God's people make is to embark on journeys too quickly. With too little promotion, only a few are able to get on board. Plan at least eight to twelve weeks in advance. This will allow time to properly prepare and promote the ministry.

Step #3. Make Plans

Choose the dates, times, and location. Meeting during a regular church gathering time may allow for one group of people to come, while meeting on another night will allow other groups to attend. One benefit of meeting on a night other than the usual church nights is that you can meet for a longer period. Ninety minutes together provides more time for discussion, study and ministry. If your session times are shorter, you can still easily get through the material by adding a few more sessions.

Step #4. Prepare to Promote Unit 1

Unit One, titled "Committing to the Call," is designed to help people hear and respond to Christ's call to follow Him and become fishers of men in our generation. It also introduces the Fishers of Men Discipleship Course and helps people make this commitment together as a team rather than trying to make the journey alone. Near the end of the unit, students are given the opportunity to respond to the Lord's call by writing and reading a letter to Jesus and the rest of the *Fishers of Men* team about their response. It is powerful. Just take the steps and watch what God will do.

A poster is provided at the end of this book. Permission is granted to make and distribute copies.

Chapter 13   Starting a Fishers of Men Group

Prepare Your Appeal

This need not be complicated at all. Simply talk about these issues:

    a. Why do you feel strongly about offering the *Fishers of Men* course?
    b. Describe how others will benefit from taking the course.
    c. Ask if there are any questions.
    d. Ask them to join you in taking Unit 1 titled, "Committing to His Call."
    e. Share the dates, time, location, cost and sign-up details.
    f. Ask them to invite others to come to the next informational meeting.
    g. Have them sign up.

Step #5. Invite other churches to start a group at the same time.

Your first reaction may be,

"Why would I want to encourage 'the competition' to get better at reaching the same people I want to reach?"

Actually, there are several benefits. First, if both groups start at the same time and come together for a mid-term progress report and have a joint celebration of everyone's progress at the end, everyone would rise to the occasion better! Why? Because they knew that their effort was being recognized by others. Secondly, it would encourage churches to support and pray for one another. Group leaders could draw strength and encouragement from each other as they embark on a common journey. Students receive a stronger sense of significance – even from another congregation - to spur them on and cheer them on. All the discipleship dynamics would be lifted to a higher level.

You can connect with other churches through friends who attend elsewhere or by asking to speak to the local Pastor's Association. The sooner you connect with them, the better. They would want adequate time to prepare. It may mean waiting a few months for them to be ready.

Another option to this concept is to start two separate groups. They may meet on different nights and locations. These groups may involve others from different churches. The dynamics would work the same.

On this issue, *Fishers of Men* deals with very basic doctrine that relates to sharing the good news of salvation through faith in Jesus Christ. Unit 7, titled "Empowered by the Spirit" is written from a charismatic and "Spirit-filled" perspective and emphasizes that we all need the promised empowering work of the Spirit to be witnesses for Christ.

Step #6. Meet with key influential people.

You know people of influence. They have many friends. People seek out their advice. Tell them about the ministry and ask them to pray about joining the cause with you. Ask them to host an informational meeting for you to invite their peers to the course.

Step #7. Host Informational Meetings

Informational meetings hosted either at church or in a home are far more influential than a bulletin announcement. It is good to have bulletin announcements and posters but relational promotion has a stronger draw than paper promotions. If people hear your heart and receive your personal invitation, they are more likely to respond.

If possible, host three identical informational meetings at different times and in different locations. This provides options and allows people the opportunity to invite friends to hear about *Fishers of Men* in the next meeting.

Step #8. Order your materials

Order the workbooks two weeks prior to your start date to assure that they arrive on time. If possible, order a few extra books in the event that someone loses theirs or a new person joins the group in the first few weeks. You may order books at http://fishersofmeninc.org/

Step #9. Make Reminder Calls

Everyone knows it. People are busy and people forget. If you and a small team make reminder calls, attendance will improve. Let people know that you value their participation and that you believe this is going to be something very good for the whole group. Your enthusiasm will help to ignite theirs.

Step #10. Begin The Series

Proper preparations will greatly increase your chances of a strong start and a good finish. May the Lord bless you as you allow Him to use you in making disciples who become fishers of men for Him.

FISHERS OF MEN
Discipleship Ministry For Relational Evangelism

UNIT 1:
COMMITTING TO HIS CALL

Learn how to join together and prepare your heart to hear and follow Christ's call to be fishers of men.

Date: _____

Time: _____

Location: _____
_____

Cost: _____

Sign up by: _____

Details:
_____
_____
_____
_____
_____
_____
_____
_____
_____
_____
_____

"Come, follow me," Jesus said, "and I will make you fishers of men."
At once they left their nets and followed Him.
Matthew 4:19-20

Sign-Up Sheet

Fishers of Men Unit 1: Committing to His Call

Start date: _____ Time: _____ Location: _____
Cost: _____ Sign-up details: _____
_____

Name	Paid	Friends who may be interested	Other notes

You likely know others who have a desire to raise up Fishers of Men for Christ. If this book helped you, please take the time to recommend it to them. Your recommendation may affect many lives for the Kingdom of God. Thanks.

-The Fishers of Men Team

http://fishersofmeninc.org/